Teachers' FAVORITE BOOKS for Kids

Teachers' Choices 1989-1993

International Reading Association
Newark, Delaware 19714, USA

TEACHERS' CHOICES
A project of the International Reading Association
Logo illustration by Chris Van Allsburg

The production of the Teachers' Choices lists that appear in this book involved many years of work by IRA's Teachers' Choices Committee. Many people in many different locations participated. In 1989 regional coordinators were Sandra Anderson (Kent, WA), Nora Forester (San Antonio, TX), Nancy Livingston (Salt Lake City, UT), Judy Long (Cumming, GA), Phyllis A. Smith (Marblehead, MA), Lynn Sygiel (Salem, MA), Judy True (Roswell, GA), V. Ellis Vance (Clovis, CA), and Lillian Webb (Worthington, OH); committee chair was Bernice E. Cullinan. In 1990 regional coordinators were Donna Bessant (Monterey, CA), Nora Forester (San Antonio, TX), Donna Harsh (Hays, KS), Nancy Livingston (Salt Lake City, UT), Judy Long (Cumming, GA), Lynn Sygiel (Salem, MA), and Lillian Webb (Worthington, OH). In 1991 regional coordinators were Donna Bessant (Monterey, CA), Lisa Johnson (San Jose, CA), Nora Forester (San Antonio, TX), Kathy Short (Tucson, AZ), Donna Harsh (Hays, KS), Karen Bihrle (Maple Grove, MN), Sherry Tavegie (Buffalo, WY), Nancy Livingston (Salt Lake City, UT), Carole Riggs (Springfield, VA), Carole Rhodes (Brooklyn, NY), Ellen M. Stepanian (Shaker Heights, OH), and Jack Humphrey (Evansville, IN). In 1992 regional coordinators were Karen Bihrle (Maple Grove, MN), Elaine Healey (Las Vegas, NV), Donald Hillyard (Evansville, IN), Lisa Johnson (San Jose, CA), Kate Kirby (Lawrenceville, GA), John Poeton (Barre, VT), Carole Riggs (Springfield, VA), Carole Rhodes (Brooklyn, NY), Kathy Short (Tucson, AZ), and Sherry Tavegie (Buffalo, WY); Dianne Monson (University of Minnesota) chaired the project. In 1993 regional coordinators were Karen Bihrle (Maple Grove, MN), Elaine Healey (Las Vegas, NV), Donald Hillyard (Evansville, IN), Sandra Imdieke (Marquette, MI), Lisa Johnson (San Jose, CA), Kate Kirby (Lawrenceville, GA), John Poeton (Barre, VT), Sam L. Sebesta (Seattle, WA), Kathy Short (Tucson, AZ), Jane Wilkins (Des Moines, IA), and Sarah Womble (Little Rock, AR); Donna Bessant (Monterey, CA) and Dianne Monson (Minneapolis, MN) coordinated the project.

ISBN 0-87207-389-0

Contents

Introduction

Chris Van Allsburg's logo, which appears opposite the contents page, vividly illustrates that Teachers' Choices are books that surprise us—they reach out and tap us on the shoulder to get our attention. These books introduce young students to ideas, issues, and questions that will set them on a path of exploration. Children and adolescents will find in these stories an unexpected wonder—they'll discover a better understanding of people and themselves.

Teachers' Favorite Books for Kids is an ideal guide for teachers who are seeking outstanding books students can enjoy in the classroom. The books included in this volume were chosen because they reflect high literary quality in style, content, structure, beauty of language, and presentation. These are books that might not be discovered or fully appreciated by children without introduction by a knowledgeable adult. Teachers will appreciate these books for their potential for use across the curriculum in areas such as language arts, social studies, math, art, drama, and music. The books offer many opportunities for reading aloud, discussion, and the stimulation of writing.

Parents will also find *Teachers' Favorite Books for Kids* a good source of suggestions for books to read aloud or share at home. Many titles provide background information on questions that arise from tours to a zoo, planetarium, or museum and from other shared family events.

Each year since 1989 the International Reading Association's Teachers' Choices project has identified outstanding U.S. trade books published for children and adolescents. These books are considered by teachers to be exceptional. The selection is accomplished through a national field test of 200 to 500 newly published books submitted by U.S. trade book publishers. Seven teams, made up of a regional coordinator, trainees, field leaders, and teacher reviewers, try out the books in classrooms and libraries to identify those that meet established criteria.

1

Regional coordinators circulate copies of the books among teachers and librarians to use with students. The coordinators record teachers' and librarians' reactions to each book and tabulate their final ratings. Every book is read by a minimum of 6 teachers or librarians in each region, although some books are read by as many as 200 people. Ratings from the seven regions are collated to produce the national list, which is published in annotated form in the November issue of *The Reading Teacher* and is reproduced and widely circulated as a separate brochure.

This volume is a compilation of Teachers' Choices lists from the past five years. Included here are descriptions of more than 150 books appropriate for children and adolescents, complete with teachers' suggestions for curriculum use, as indicated by the symbol ❦. In order to make the book easier to use, entries are grouped into Primary (K-2, age 5-8), Intermediate (Grades 3-5, age 8-11), and Advanced (Grades 6-8, age 11-14) levels. Of course, these categories do overlap. Each entry includes bibliographic information about the book and an annotation; the Teachers' Choices list on which the book first appeared is indicated by the initials TC followed by the year. (Please note that the publishers' names and ISBNs refer to the original publications—hardcovers, except where indicated—evaluated at the test sites. In many cases, particularly for books from the earliest lists, paperback editions may now be available; in some cases, the original edition may be difficult to find or out of print. Librarians and bookstore employees should be able to provide current information on the availability of particular books. The bibliographic information here is provided simply as a starting point.) To increase the collection's usefulness as a resource tool, we have included indexes of titles, authors, and illustrators.

This volume is a wonderful source for teachers, librarians, parents, grandparents, and young readers alike. Let *Teachers' Favorite Books for Kids* surprise you. You'll discover some outstanding books for kids!

Primary

(Grades K-2)

All Those Secrets of the World
Jane Yolen. Illustrated by Leslie Baker. Little, Brown. ISBN 0-316-96891-9. TC '92.

This recollection of an event remembered from childhood is beautifully illustrated with watercolors that evoke the 1940s. When their father sails away to war, Janie and her 5-year-old brother, Michael, explore their own world. Janie is especially fascinated when she recognizes that the farther away you are, the smaller you seem to be.

❧ The story is a natural springboard for describing experiences children remember with pleasure. Some children chose to tell about those special times; others preferred to illustrate them and then supply the written text. They were encouraged to include descriptions of sounds and smells as well as sights.

The Art Lesson
Tomie dePaola. Illustrated by the author. Putnam. ISBN 0-399-21688-X. TC '90.

Remember entering school eager to learn everything and knowing what everything should be? Tomie dePaola learned to be creative in drawing pictures at home; he shares his disappointment with the rules and constraints imposed in his school art class. He is rescued by an art teacher who recognizes and nurtures his talent.

❧ This book led to discussions of school rules, teacher-child interactions, and how a child's interests can lead to a career. It was used in an "All About Me" social studies unit and in writing process classrooms as a model of autobiographical and memory writing. It led to comparisons with the art in dePaola's other books.

At the Crossroads

Rachel Isadora. Illustrated by the author. Greenwillow. ISBN 0-688-05270-3. TC '92.

Anticipation and celebration radiate from young faces as South African children await their fathers' return home after 10 months of working in the mines. Dancing, singing, and music-making are the order of the day, and the crowd swells and then dwindles as the hours of waiting go by. The simple text and moving illustrations capture the universal joy of family reunions while also depicting the hardships of life in segregated townships.

❧ Children discussed preparations for their own family reunions and compared them with the preparations portrayed in the book. Families across cultures were compared to point up the similarities. Living conditions in the segregated townships in South Africa were contrasted with living conditions of the students.

Aunt Flossie's Hats (and Crab Cakes Later)

Elizabeth Fitzgerald Howard. Illustrated by James Ransome. Clarion Books. ISBN 0-395-54682-6. TC '92.

Beautiful illustrations enhance this story that explores the special relationship between an aunt and her two nieces. As they try on Aunt Flossie's many hats, the three share stories about the events that transpired when Flossie wore the hats.

❧ Readers were encouraged to investigate their family history and create hats that helped tell the oral stories. They interviewed members of their families and wrote collections detailing the oral traditions and history. Intergenerational relationships were extended and encouraged.

Illustration copyright © 1991 by Charles Mikolaycak. From Bearhead: A
Russian Folktale *by Eric A. Kimmel. Used by permission of Holiday House.*

Bearhead: A Russian Folktale
Adapted by Eric A. Kimmel. Illustrated by Charles Mikolaycak.
Holiday House. ISBN 0-8234-0902-3. TC '92.

> Using tongue-in-cheek humor, this Russian folk tale illus-
> trates the humorous side of one of the noble bears of folk
> literature. Bearhead, an unusual character with the head of a
> bear and the body of a man, uses his cleverness to outwit
> the evil witch, Madame Hexaba.
>
> ❧ When teachers read this book aloud to the students,
> they discovered the fun of the story and found that it can be
> compared to many American folk tales.

Cactus Hotel

Brenda Z. Guiberson. Illustrated by Megan Lloyd. Henry Holt. ISBN 0-8050-1333-4. TC '92.

This hotel is 50 feet high and weighs eight tons! Over a life span of up to 200 years, the giant saguaro cactus offers shelter to a wealth of desert-dwelling fauna. The journey from germinating seed to fully developed "cactus hotel" is charted in language that is easy to understand and pictures that help young readers envision the life cycle of the giant cactus and the symbiotic relationship of animals and cactus.

🐛 The book is a natural for introducing desert life to children. One class made a desert mural with a large painted saguaro cactus. Holes were cut in the cactus, and "hotel guests" were pinned in the holes. As children dramatized the book, the "guests" were moved around. Desert animals were classified by species and then studied in more detail. The book was compared to *The Great Kapok Tree* by Lynne Cherry (a 1991 Teachers' Choices title).

Dragonfly's Tale

Kristina Rodanas, reteller. Illustrated by the author. Clarion. ISBN 0-395-57003-4. TC '93.

This retelling, based on a Zuni tale, is set long ago in the American Southwest and details a "wasteful" festival that upsets the Corn Maidens. The blessing of a bountiful harvest is withdrawn by the spirits and the tribe must leave the village. In their haste, they leave behind a sleeping brother and sister. To soothe his sister's fears, the boy creates a cornstalk dragonfly that flies off to tell the Corn Maidens about the young ones. Valuing the children's previous offer of food, the Corn Maidens return bounty to the land, and the tribe learns a contemporary lesson about waste.

🐛 This tale is ideal for retelling. In the prologue, the author tells the origin of the tale and the fact that she adds information. In a multicultural investigation, use this book to show the value of oral story cultures. Also appropriate for **Intermediate**.

Dream Wolf
Paul Goble, reteller. Illustrated by the author. Bradbury. ISBN 0-02-736585-9. TC '91.

A kindly wolf comes to the aid of two lost children, Tiblio and Tankis, when they wander away while gathering berries. Goble retells and illustrates the Plains Indian legend in glowing detail.

🍎 This excellent book enriched a social studies unit on the Plains Indians and language arts focus on legends. A good read-aloud book.

The Empty Pot
Demi. Illustrated by the author. Henry Holt. ISBN 0-8050-1217-6. TC '91.

Ping, a Chinese boy, loves flowers; anything he plants grows. To select an heir to the throne, the Emperor gives a seed to each child in the kingdom and asks that the plants be brought back a year later. Unbeknownst to the children, the seeds have been cooked so that they won't germinate. When Ping is the only child courageous enough to present an empty pot to the Emperor, he is chosen heir to the throne.

🍎 The book was used in a study of values, honesty, and courage. It became a model for coordinating artwork with text in the study of literature. An excellent read-aloud.

Encounter
Jane Yolen. Illustrated by David Shannon. HBJ. ISBN 0-15-225962-7. TC '93.

A controversial book, one of few published during the Columbus Quincentenary that took the perspective of the Native Americans whose land Columbus "discovered." The story is told through the eyes of a Taino boy whose dreams have made him uneasy about his people's encounter with men who look like parrots in bright clothing. Despite his warning, the men are welcomed and the Tainos' lands and lives are lost.

🍎 Children found this book thought provoking and made comparisons with other books about the Columbus event

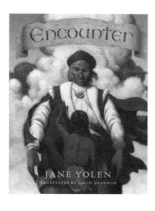

such as Peter Sis's *Follow the Dream.* The end notes led them to further research using *The Tainos* by Francine Jacobs and *Morning Girl* by Michael Dorris. They also compared this book to more recent books about cultural encounters such as *Angel Child, Dragon Child* by Michele Surat. Also appropriate for **Intermediate** and **Advanced.**

Eric Carle's Animals Animals

Compiled by Laura Whipple. Illustrated by Eric Carle. Philomel. ISBN 0-399-21744-4. TC '90.

A collection of 62 poems by a variety of poets describes the peculiarities of wild and domestic animals. Eric Carle illustrated the anthology with colored tissue paper and paint collages that show the wonder and diversity of the animal world.

✾ Children savored the brilliant art and poetry. Later, for science, they categorized reptiles, fish, birds, and mammals; discussed ecology, endangered species, and natural habitats. They compared the poetic characterizations of animals with other sources of information. In language arts, they created choral readings for two voices, listed animal-related figurative language, researched the folklore of proverbs, and wrote haiku, limericks, and other pattern poems modeled in the anthology.

Feathers for Lunch

Lois Ehlert. Illustrated by the author. HBJ. ISBN 0-15-230550-5. TC '91.

Only the cat's tail shows on the first page to arouse our anticipation. Soon we learn that because the cat wears a bell to warn the birds of his presence, all he catches are "feathers for lunch." Vivid collage illustrations and rhymed text present a satisfying story.

🍎 Teachers used this book in a science unit focusing on birds. The glossary stimulated discussions of the food birds consume, types of homes they build, and areas in which they live. Local Audubon Society members visited classrooms to stimulate interest in ornithology as a hobby. The illustrations became a model for art lessons.

Fly Away Home
Eve Bunting. Illustrated by Ronald Himler. Clarion. ISBN 0-395-55962-6. TC '92.

A young boy tells the story of the life he and his father lead as homeless people living at a large airport. Andrew shares the "rules" one needs to follow to remain unnoticed—their key to survival—as he clearly describes the cautious routine of their homeless existence. The soft watercolor illustrations help make this book an inviting experience.

🍎 The book was used at different grade levels to focus on homelessness in U.S. society. One first-grade teacher used the KWL strategy to facilitate learning: what we Know, what we Want to learn, and what we Learned about homeless people in the community and throughout the country.

Forest of Dreams
Rosemary Wells. Illustrated by Susan Jeffers. Dial Books for Young Readers. ISBN 0-8037-0570-0. TC '89.

In a gentle mood piece written in verse, a child extols the praises of God for the gifts given her and the beauty of nature from snowy winter to a flowery spring. Susan Jeffers, in her first oil paintings in any book, captures the text's sensitive meaning by filling the opening endpapers with evocative snow lined trees that gradually change through the pages into ones filled with glorious blossoms on the closing endpapers.

❧ This book became the impetus for art lessons, dramatization, and discussing the concept of changing seasons. We savor the sheer beauty of its illustrations and appreciation of nature.

A Frog Prince

Alix Berenzy. Illustrated by the author. Henry Holt. ISBN 0-8050-0426-2. TC '90.

Spurned by the princess, a heartbroken frog sets out to find someone who will love him just as he is. Berenzy replaces the ending of the traditional Grimm's "The Frog Prince" with this version told from the frog's point of view. Eventually, the frog finds another princess, a sleeping frog, who responds to his kiss.

❧ Teachers read this book aloud and students searched for similarities and differences in other versions of "The Frog Prince." Students rewrote the story as a Readers Theatre script and presented it in dramatic form.

Going West

Jean Van Leeuwen. Illustrated by Thomas B. Allen. Dial. ISBN 0-8037-1027-5. TC '93.

The story is narrated effectively by 7-year-old Hannah as she describes her pioneer family's move out west. Hardships and danger are nicely balanced with family warmth, love, and survival skills. The description of the family's feelings in the unsettled land, especially loneliness and isolation, makes the story believable. The subdued, hazy, pastel drawings enhance and strengthen the text.

🐾 Teachers used this book in a unit on the westward expansion to emphasize American pioneer life and survival skills. Students experimented with the artist's technique, using brown butcher paper, colored chalk, and hand smudging.

The Great Kapok Tree: A Tale of the Amazon Rain Forest

Lynne Cherry. Illustrated by the author. HBJ. ISBN 0-15-200520-X. TC '91.

Animals of the Amazon rain forest persuade a man not to chop down their home in the great Kapok tree; their message portrays the interdependence of nature. A strong conservation theme is conveyed through flowing text and lush illustrations.

🐾 This text stimulated discussions about our need to protect the earth's environment in a study of ecology. Students conducted research on rain forests, animals who live in them, and what we can do to protect them. Students also used the book's maps to locate geographic regions of rain forests.

Great Northern Driver: The Loon

Barbara Juster Esbensen. Illustrated by Mary Barrett Brown. Little, Brown. ISBN 0-316-4954-8. TC '91.

This book traces the spectacular story of one of the most interesting and elusive of all North American birds, the loon. Following its seasonal cycle, readers learn about the loon's size, mating habits, care for its young, and problems of survival.

🦋 Students searched for pictorial information on this primitive bird's ancestors. They used graphic organizers to compare the loon with other birds, listing habitat, food, coloring, enemies, and special traits.

A House for Hermit Crab

Eric Carle. Illustrated by the author. Picture Book Studio. ISBN 0-88708-056-1. TC '89.

A hermit crab outgrows his old shell, moves into a new one, and decorates it with sea creatures he meets in his travels. In a delightful combination of fact and feeling, the text follows the hermit crab through a year's migration while the collage illustrations take the reader on a visual underwater tour of sea creatures and scenery.

🦋 The story line naturally stimulates language arts and science discussions about moving, changing, and adapting to new environments. An accompanying teacher's guide outlines ideas for a thematic approach to living and learning.

Illustrations by Jane Breskin Zalben copyright © 1992 by Jane Breskin Zalben. From Inner Chimes: Poems and Poetry, *selected by Bobbye S. Goldstein. Reprinted by permission of Wordsong, Boyds Mills Press.*

Inner Chimes: Poems on Poetry
Bobbye S. Goldstein. Illustrated by Jane Breskin Zalben.
Wordsong/Boyds Mills. ISBN 1-56397-040-6. TC '93.

A delightful anthology of poetry about poetry compiled by
a New York educator. Many of the poets are contemporary
children's favorites, and many poems were written especially for this book. The words, rhymes, and rhythmic language linguistically illustrate many positive emotions and
the frustrations of writing poetry.

🐛 Topics and styles of the poems included make excellent
"large print" charts to enrich a print environment. Various
styles of poems may serve as excellent models for student-
written poetry. Outstanding material for teachers to read
aloud to begin daily poetry sharing. Also appropriate for
Intermediate.

Is Your Mama a Llama?
Deborah Guarino. Illustrated by Steven Kellogg. Scholastic. ISBN
0-590-41387-2. TC '90.

A whimsical guessing game in which a baby llama asks his
animal friends, "Is your mama a llama?" Their response, a
rhyming description of their mother, gives the answer on
the following page. Kellogg's full color illustrations of animals in their natural habitat are full of humor.

🐛 Teachers heard "Read it again!" after each read-aloud
session. Children joined in to sing out the rhymes and answers in chorus. They compared this book with an old favorite, *Are You My Mother?* by P.D. Eastman, and wrote
their own riddles about animal mothers. Because of the pre-
dictable and rhythmic language, the book served as excellent material for shared reading sessions.

John Tabor's Ride
Edward C. Day. Illustrated by Dirk Zimmer. Knopf. ISBN 394-
98577-X. TC '90.

This tall tale is based on an 1846 book of whaling adventures originally kept as a seaman's journal. Brash young
John Tabor complains about everything on his first whaling
voyage until one night a mysterious old man appears and

13

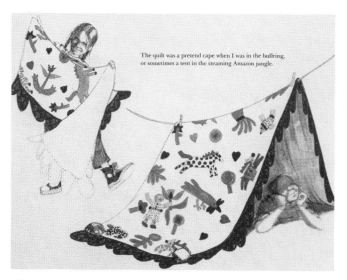

The quilt was a pretend cape when I was in the bullring, or sometimes a tent in the steaming Amazon jungle.

Illustration copyright © 1988 by Patricia Polacco from The Keeping Quilt. *Reprinted by permission of the publisher, Simon & Schuster Books for Young Readers, New York.*

takes him for a fantastic ride on the back of a whale. Happy to return alive, John becomes the most jolly whaler in the fleet. Zimmer's auburn, green, and blue watercolors with detailed cross hatching extend the feeling of a tall tale.

🐚 Perfect for reading aloud, this story led to a study of other tall tales. John Tabor's constant grumbling became vivid dialogue in Readers Theatre scripts. Students compared Tabor's complaints to their own.

The Keeping Quilt

Patricia Polacco. Illustrated by the author. Simon and Schuster. ISBN 0-671-64963-9. TC '89.

Long ago, Polacco's quilt was made from relatives' cast-off clothing and bordered with her great grandma Anna's babushka which came from "backhome Russia." The quilt becomes an integral part of important family celebrations: It serves as a wedding huppa, tablecloth, baby cover, and comforter for tired old legs. Soft black and white illustrations, enlivened by the colorfully appliqued and bordered

quilt, show how the quilt is used by succeeding generations.

💝 This book stimulated discussions of family heirlooms,
their part in family traditions, and the meaning of cultural
heritage.

The Legend of the Indian Paintbrush

Retold by Tomie dePaola. Illustrated by the author. G.P.
Putnam's Sons. ISBN 0-399-32534-4. TC '89.

Little Gopher, smaller than other boys of his Plains Indian
tribe, cannot do what others do, although he discovers he
has a different talent. He paints pictures of tribal glories,
but capturing the colors of the evening sky eludes his skill.
One night a voice leads him to a special place where he
finds brushes filled with the colors he desires. After paint-
ing the perfect picture, he leaves the paintbrushes on the
ground and returns the next day to find they have taken
root; they have become flowers that we now call Indian
Paintbrush.

💝 We compared this book with *The Legend of the Bluebonnet*
(Tomie dePaola, Putnam, 1983), discussed Indian legends,
and traced the folklore underlying some of the flowers in
our state.

Let the Celebrations Begin!

Margaret Wild. Illustrated by Julie Vivas. Orchard. ISBN 0-531-
05937-5. TC '92.

In a World War II concentration camp, Sarah, a young
Jewish girl, remembers the days when she had food, her
own bedroom, her own bed, and even her own toys. Miriam
and the other women in the camp are busily making toys
for a very special party to be held at the war's end.

💝 This book led to a discussion about how fortunate we
are. Children learned how difficult it is for many people to
have those special things that we take for granted.

The Magic School Bus Inside the Human Body

Joanna Cole. Illustrated by Bruce Degen. Scholastic. ISBN 0-590-41426-7. TC '90.

> After Ms. Frizzle introduces the study of the human body and takes her students to visit a science museum, Arnold inadvertently swallows the magic school bus. This gives the skeptical scientists a first-hand look at the major parts of the human body.
>
> 🍎 Teachers introduced science and health concepts and encouraged students to research a particular area. Students took notes and discussed different ways to learn; they compared information in this book with that found in their textbooks. They compared bodily functions to ordinary household objects and used the basic story idea for creative writing about digestion from the point of view of the food.

Mandy

Barbara D. Booth. Illustrated by Jim LaMarche. Lothrop, Lee & Shepard. ISBN 0-688-10338-3. TC '92.

> Mandy's world of quietness is filled with her curiosity of what sounds might be like. She learns to rely on her other senses to know when her grandmother's chocolate chip cookies are done, how to dance with music from the radio, and whether her grandmother is feeling happy. The story will remind children of special memories they share with a grandparent as well as open their minds to the world of a deaf child.
>
> 🍎 This story, rich with images and sensory detail, can be used as a springboard into what makes a good piece of writing. Children discovered how difficult it was to write a favorite childhood memory without the sense of sounds, hearing, or talking.

My Great-Aunt Arizona

Gloria Houston. Illustrated by Susan Condie Lamb. HarperCollins. ISBN 0-06-022606-4. TC '93.

> The one-room schoolhouse in the Appalachian Mountains was the magical place a young teacher used to focus generations of children's thoughts on the places they would go one

Illustration by Jim LaMarche from Barbara D. Booth's Mandy. *Text copyright © 1991 by Barbara D. Booth. Illustration copyright © 1991 by Jim LaMarche. Reprinted by permission of Lothrop, Lee & Shepard Books, a division of William Morrow & Company, Inc.*

day. Arizona Houston did not make those journeys herself, but she helped children believe in the possibilities in their lives. Teachers will surely enjoy sharing a book that reveals the joy and contribution of their profession.

🍎 Children can compare a "then and now" view of education as well as respond to some reasons for change in the structure of schools.

Osa's Pride

Ann Grifalconi. Illustrated by the author. Little, Brown. ISBN 0-316-32865-0. TC '91.

> Osa, from *The Village of Round and Square Houses* and *Darkness and the Butterfly,* returns in a story about the dangers of pride. Osa alienates friends who tire of her fictitious stories about her "heroic" father.

17

❦ This book became a model in a study of concise character description. Readers became writers as they recounted personal experiences in which pride proved to be a help or a hindrance to them. They compared and contrasted elements of Osa's pride with that of characters from other books.

Princess Furball

Retold by Charlotte Huck. Illustrated by Anita Lobel. Greenwillow. ISBN 0-688-07838-9. TC '90.

In a variant of the Cinderella story, a princess grows to be strong, capable, and clever, besides being beautiful. When her father promises her in marriage to an ogre, she demands impossible bridal gifts: dresses as golden as the sun, as silvery as the moon, as glittering as the stars, and a fur coat made of skins from a thousand animals. Shocked that her father delivers the gifts, she runs away. A neighboring king discovers her true nature and marries her. Naturally they live happily ever after.

🍎 Teachers used this book in social studies discussions of self-concept and the various roles women and men can assume. It became part of a study of the Middle Ages and showed the hardships necessary to provide food and shelter. Primarily, it was enjoyed as a read aloud and compared to other Cinderella variants.

Rain Player

David Wisniewski. Illustrated by the author. Clarion. ISBN 0-395-55112-9. TC '92.

Pik, a young Mayan boy, is an expert at playing pok-a-tok (a combination of basketball and soccer). During a drought, he challenges Choc, a Mayan god, to a game. With the help of a jaguar, a quetzal, and cenote (water), Pik wins and the drought comes to an end.

🍎 Art students studied the spectacular cut-paper illustrations done by Wisniewski. History classes studied the Mayan culture and its impact upon present day Mexico, Belize, Honduras, Guatemala, and El Salvador. Drought and its consequences on agriculture, people, and political policies also became issues for discussion.

The Rough-Face Girl

Rafe Martin. Illustrated by David Shannon. Putnam. ISBN 0-399-21859-9. TC '93.

From the Algonquin Indian tradition, this Cinderella variant stresses the beauty of nature and the beauty within us. Hoping to marry the invisible being, two vain and arrogant sisters fail to describe the invisible being as proof that they can see him. Their sister, the rough-face girl, her face and body scarred from having to sit and tend the fire, is successful because she sees the beauty of the invisible being in the nature around her.

🍎 Teachers judged this a worthy addition to studies of Indian lore and Cinderella variants. Children noted the importance of nature and the author's use of natural detail such as the birch bark dress and buckskin moccasins. Also appropriate for **Intermediate** and **Advanced**.

The Rumor of Pavel and Paali: A Ukrainian Folktale

Adapted by Carol Kismaric. Illustrated by Charles Mikolaycak. Harper and Row. ISBN 0-06-023278-1. TC '89.

Cruel, stingy Pavel exacts a harsh price from his gentle twin brother, Paali, when he wins a wager. Pavel robs Paali of his worldly goods and eventually of his eyesight. Blinded, Paali wanders into the Great Forest, overhears the remedies to ills cast by evil spirits, and unwittingly sets in motion Pavel's destruction.

🍎:The vivid struggle between good and evil led to discussions of values in our society—sour versus happy, sacrifice versus retribution, greed versus generosity, right versus wrong. Students quickly translated the ancient moral to relevant topics of today—income tax, advertising, truthfulness. We also studied the folkloric cycle of three events and the retribution given to the evil one. We learned about folklore and social studies through a powerful story.

Sami and the Time of the Troubles

Florence Parry Heide and Judith Heide Gilliland. Illustrated by Ted Lewin. Clarion. ISBN: 0-395-55964-2. TC '93.

The terror of civil war in Lebanon is revealed through the eyes of Sami, a 10-year-old boy. With sharp contrasts of light and color, the illustrations take the reader deeper into the conflict of life between nightly bomb attacks. Hope is the gift Sami's grandfather passes to him to carry them all beyond "the time of troubles."

🍎 This strong story can help children understand the continuing Middle East conflict as well as feel empathy for children and families who suffer and struggle in the midst of war. Through written responses, children may realize that their voices can be the sound of hope for the future. Also appropriate for **Intermediate.**

Seven Blind Mice

Ed Young. Illustrated by the author. Philomel. ISBN 0-399-22261-8. TC '93.

Ed Young's stunning paper-collage illustrations bring alive this ancient fable of seven blind mice who one by one inves-

Illustration copyright © 1992 by Ted Lewin, Clarion Books, from Sami and the Time of the Troubles.

tigate the strange "something" by their pond. Because each examines only part of the elephant, they come back with different ideas until the last mouse ventures out and examines the whole.

🐭 Children read this book on many different levels. Some connected with the message about wisdom and the need to look at the whole instead of getting lost in the parts. Others were intrigued with the illustrations and experimented with collage. Others were interested in Young's use of color and the reasons why the last mouse was white. Young readers also used the book as a way to explore colors, the days of the week, and ordinal numbers. Also appropriate for **Intermediate.**

Sing a Song of Popcorn

Selected by Beatrice Schenk de Regniers, Eva Moore, Mary Michaels White, and Jan Carr. Illustrated by Marcia Brown, Leo Dillon, Diane Dillon, Richard Egielski, Trina Schart Hyman, Maurice Sendak, Marc Simont, and Margot Zemach. Scholastic. ISBN 0-590-40645-0. TC '89.

This collection of 128 poems provides busy classroom teachers with poems that are surefire hits. Selections grouped under nine subject headings (for example, Spooky Poems, Mostly Animals) are illustrated by winners of the Caldecott Medal.

🍎 Teachers read and reread these poems aloud; they also copied some onto large chart paper so students could read along, memorize, or dramatize ones they loved. Children chose poems to memorize and began their own poetry collections by recording favorites and writing their own.

The Star Maiden: An Ojibway Tale
Barbara Juster Esbensen. Illustrated by Helen K. Davie. Little, Brown. ISBN 0-316-24951-3. TC '89.

This pourquoi story retells the Ojibway Indian legend of the maiden who tires of the sky. She experiments with many earthly transformations but concludes with satisfaction that she best resembles the blossoms of the water lily.

🍎 We introduced Native American folklore and the concept of retelling with additions and changes made by the storyteller. The author's note helped us to track primary source material, to locate other versions, and to juxtapose the original story with its variants. Students focused on the details of the illustrations, noting that each picture contained the action of the text, the artistic representation of Chippewa designs as a border, and the anchoring of the illustration with a small horizontal watercolor including the environment and native animals.

Storm in the Night
Mary Stolz. Illustrated by Pat Cummings. Harper and Row. ISBN 0-06-025913-2. TC '89.

While sitting through a frightening thunderstorm that has put the lights out, Thomas hears a story from his grandfather's boyhood—when Grandfather was afraid of thunderstorms.

🍎 This book led to discussions of fears—of the dark, of storms, of being alone, and of the comforting presence of a grandparent. It also led to talking about caring for pets and being responsible for another creature's welfare. Students savored the iridescent illustrations and noted that the illus-

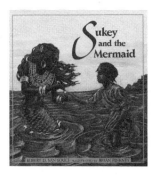

© 1992 by Brian Pinkney.

trator combined both the past and present by inserting small vignettes of Grandfather and Thomas when featuring events showing Grandfather as a child. They adapted the technique into their own artwork.

Sukey and the Mermaid

Robert D. San Souci. Illustrated by Brian Pinkney. Four Winds. ISBN 0-02-778141-0. TC '93.

This Afro-Caribbean folktale features a young girl named Sukey, a lonely, overworked child who is harassed by her lazy stepfather. One day she runs off to the seashore and encounters a beautiful, brown-skinned, black-eyed mermaid. In a captivating tale, Sukey is rescued from her miserable life and experiences the wonders below the sea. She returns home later and encounters more trials with her family, but in the end all is well in Sukey's world. The rhythmic, buoyant language used in this magical story is enhanced with wonderful scratchboard line illustrations.

🍎 Teachers used this book in studying folktales of various cultures.

Thirteen Moons on Turtle's Back

Joseph Bruchac and Jonathan London, retellers. Illustrated by Thomas Locker. Philomel. ISBN 0-399-22141-7. TC '93.

In many Native American cultures, each of the 13 moons of the year has its own story and name. Abenaki storyteller Bruchac and poet London present stories from 13 tribes.

Locker's oil paintings enrich the 13 tales. A good resource to incorporate multicultural activities throughout the year.

🍒 Students did further studies of the Native American cultures mentioned. They researched other legends and created a legend to explain a natural occurrence in their own desert environment (unusual snow in the desert valley, natural hot springs). They also made comparisons to the year and to the modern calendar. Also appropriate for **Intermediate.**

Thunder Cake
Patricia Polacco. Illustrated by the author. Philomel. ISBN 0-399-22231-6. TC '91.

Grandmother distracts a child who is frightened by a threatening thunderstorm by asking her to collect all the ingredients to bake a special family cake. Colorful Russian folk art images.

🍒 Since the recipe was provided, the natural follow-up was to bake the cake. Students also made lists of things that frightened them and wrote about ways they overcame their fears.

Totem Pole
Diane Hoyt-Goldsmith. Illustrated with photos by Lawrence Migdale. Holiday House. ISBN 0-8234-0809-4. TC '91.

A photo essay examines the life of a boy whose Native American father carves a totem pole in the style of his Tsimshian tribe. The boy is proud of his heritage as he watches his father take a log from the forest and release different animal spirits from it as he carves.

🍒 This book was used in Native American studies to highlight oral history and tribal traditions. Art classes and woodworking classes used the art forms shown to experiment with woodcarving.

Up North at the Cabin
Marsha W. Chall. Illustrated by Steve Johnson. Lothrop, Lee & Shepard. ISBN 0-688-09732-4. TC '93.

Illustration from Up North at the Cabin © *1992 by Marsha Wilson Chall, illustrations by Steve Johnson. Reprinted by permission from Lothrop, Lee & Shepard, a division of William Morrow & Co.*

The young female narrator describes her beautiful memories of vacations in a northern cabin and in the process discovers her source of bravery, risk taking, and strong family support. The illustrations gracefully supplement a soothing text.

❧ A class discussion of how family supports risk taking would be appropriate with this story. A diary of family memoirs with extended family members adds to the story. A study of the role of words and illustrations could be an

excellent extension of this book. Also appropriate for
Intermediate.

Urban Roosts: Where Birds Nest in the City
Barbara Bash. Illustrated by the author. Sierra Club/Little,
Brown. ISBN 0-316-08306-2. TC '91.

> A variety of birds—including barn owls, finches, house
> wrens, and peregrine falcons—roost in the heart of the city
> where they thrive amid glass and concrete.
>
> 🍀 Units on ecology, adaptation and change, birds, city
> life, and country life grew from this book. Both text and il-
> lustrations provided comparisons of bird life, city nesting
> areas, and survival. Students throughout the elementary
> grades located birds in their neighborhoods, wrote journals
> about their observations, researched facts and compared in-
> formation, and wrote reports and books.

Vasilissa the Beautiful
Elizabeth Winthrop, adapter. Illustrated by Alexander Koshkin.
HarperCollins. ISBN 0-06-021662-X. TC '92.

> This Russian folk tale has several themes that children will
> find familiar: the death of Vasilissa's mother; a mean step-
> mother and two stepsisters who try to get rid of her by
> sending her into the forest to get fire from the witch Baba
> Yaga; and the good Vasilissa's marriage to the Tsar. The
> magnificent illustrations make Baba Yaga's area of the for-
> est delightfully creepy.
>
> 🍀 This was a good tale for dramatizing. Older students
> rewrote it as a Readers Theatre script. One group compared
> it to other folk tales they knew, and this led to listening to
> two other Vasilissa stories and several Baba Yaga stories.

A Visit to Oma
Marisabina Russo. Illustrated by the author. Greenwillow. ISBN
0-688-09623-9. TC '92.

> This touching book highlights a very special relationship
> between Oma and her great-granddaughter, Celeste. Since

they do not speak the same language, Celeste conjures up a story that she thinks Oma is telling.

🍎 This book helped foster intergenerational connections. Students began to explore their family history. They embarked on journeys through their elders' past as they detailed and recorded real and imaginary adventures.

The Wall

Eve Bunting. Illustrated by Ronald Himler. Clarion. ISBN 0-395-51588-2. TC '91.

This is a moving account of a father and son searching for the name of the boy's grandfather on the Vietnam Veterans' memorial in Washington, D.C. The boy, who never knew his grandfather, wishes he was there as he watches another grandfather and grandson.

🍎 This poignant story made history come alive for students. They compared the book with other stories dealing with the ravages of war, such as *My Hiroshima* and *Potatoes Potatoes*.

The Wednesday Surprise

Eve Bunting. Illustrated by Donald Carrick. Clarion. ISBN 0-89919-721-3. TC '90.

Anna and her Grandma cook up a marvelous birthday surprise for Anna's father. In preparation for his party, they read together each Wednesday evening while they are home alone. When it is time for the surprise, Grandma reads aloud from the books she and Anna shared, and only then do we realize that Grandma is the one who has learned to read.

🍎 The surprise ending opens discussion on the value of learning to read at any age. Cross-age reading sessions followed. Young children described gifts they shared with older people. Intergenerational literacy programs celebrated the joy of shared learning.

The Whales' Song

Dyan Sheldon. Illustrated by Gary Blythe. Dial. ISBN 0-8037-0972-2. TC '92.

> Have you ever thought whales could sing or that they had a special gift to share with you? Lilly's grandmother shares her magical childhood memories of whales with Lilly, and Lilly's own special moment with the whales at the seashore is filled with wonder and awe. A song can be heard by those who believe.
>
> 🐋 The story lends itself to several comparisons: the character contrast between Lilly's grandmother and skeptical Great Uncle Frederick; respect for nature as contrasted with thoughtless waste of living things; and fact versus fantasy. The book would fit naturally into a unit on oceans or endangered species.

Why the Sky Is Far Away: A Nigerian Folktale

Mary-Joan Gerson, reteller. Illustrated by Carla Golembe. Joy Street/Little, Brown. ISBN 0-316-30852-8. TC '93.

> Once the sky was so near that all people had to do was reach up, take a piece of sky, and eat it. This cautionary tale, told in bold language and brash pastels, explains what went wrong. An author's note reminds us that this 500-year-old Bini story has modern implications.
>
> 🐋 Talk about it—why would people have composed this tale and passed it down across the years? Together, compose a modern version. Write it and illustrate it boldly. Post its pages for modern people to read and heed! Also appropriate for **Intermediate.**

The Year of the Perfect Christmas Tree

Gloria Houston. Illustrated by Barbara Cooney. Dial Books for Young Readers. ISBN 0-8037-0330-7. TC '89.

> Before Ruthie's Papa leaves for World War I, he picks out the special balsam tree they will contribute to the village church for its holiday celebration. When he has not returned, Ruthie and Mama trek across the snowy Appalachian countryside to cut the tree and haul it to the

church. In a tender final scene, Papa waits on the church steps reaching out to embrace his family.

🍎 Teachers read this book aloud, rewrote the text as a Readers Theatre script, and presented the story in dramatic form. We drew a timeline to place the events of the story in history.

Yonder

Tony Johnston. Illustrated by Lloyd Bloom. Dial Books for Young Readers. ISBN 0-8037-0278-7. TC '89.

A young farmer plants a plum tree to commemorate his marriage. The tree grows and each year fills the sky with pink clouds of blossoms for three generations as his family continues to mark major events by planting another tree, including one at his death. The poetic text rings of a life cycle folk song and the impressionistic illustrations celebrate the meaning and beauty of life.

🍎 Teachers read this book aloud time and again until students took over the reading. Students begged to take this book to other classes to read aloud and to share the unusual majesty of this story.

Young Lions

Toshi Yoshida. Illustrated by the author. Philomel. ISBN 0-399-21546-8. TC '90.

Three young lions set out to discover their world on the African plains and come upon rhinoceros, water buffaloes, zebras, impalas, cheetahs, vultures, hyenas, and gnus. At the edge of Mt. Kilimanjaro, they watch hundreds of animals gather to feed at twilight. The understated, true-to-life story allows us to observe animals of the wilds.

🍎 Teachers used this in a special unit on Africa and animals of Africa; they compared information about the various species.

Intermediate
(Grades 3-5)

Arms and Armor
Michele Byam. Illustrated with photographs by Dave King.
Alfred A. Knopf Books for Young Readers. ISBN 0-394-99622-4.
TC '89.

> This beautifully crafted informational book depicts the design and uses of hand weapons and armor from 300,000 B.C. to the early 20th century.
>
> 🐾 The book led to class discussions on how the development of weapons has paralleled and influenced history. One group created an arms timeline; another compared weapons found in different geographic regions of the world. Students drew maps and placed drawings of the weapons at the site of their origin.

Bears
Ian Stirling. Illustrated with photos and drawings. Sierra Club.
ISBN 0-87156-574-9. TC '93.

> The origins, evolution, habitats, behavior, and life cycles of the eight present-day species of bears are discussed. This is an excellent reference, featuring more than 40 color photographs.
>
> 🐾 Graphic organizers were used to compare bears of different geographical areas. Students also created models of a

variety of bear habitats. Some students read folktales featuring bears and discussed why bears are portrayed as they are.

Behind Rebel Lines: The Incredible Story of Emma Edmonds, Civil War Spy

Seymour Reit. Gulliver/HBJ. ISBN 9-15-200416-5. TC '89.

Canadian-born Emma Edmonds (1841-1898) disguises herself as a man and joins the Union Army in 1861. As a spy, Emma infiltrates the rebel lines of the Confederate Army of Northern Virginia to bring back information to her adopted leaders.

🐛 Students drew maps to show Emma's route from Canada, Michigan, Washington D.C., Virginia, and Illinois. Others traced stories of the 200 women who served as men during the Civil War. Some extended the diary format by writing entries about Emma for a specific date. Others wrote a letter from Emma disguised as Private Thompson. Some compared events reported here with factual accounts in history books.

Beyond the Ridge

Paul Goble. Illustrated by the author. Bradbury. ISBN 0-02-736581-6. TC '90.

The Plains Indians' view of death is depicted in this moving story of an old woman's departure from this world and her journey beyond the ridge into a land of wonder and beauty, the Land of Many Tipis. Goble's illustrations help us see beyond the ridge into an unknown world.

🐛 The poems and prayers as well as the story stimulated a discussion of death and the possibility of life after death. Comparisons were made between what the Indian family did after a death and what others do after a loved one dies. Students studied Plains Indians' customs and beliefs.

The Big Book for Peace

Edited by Ann Durell and Marilyn Sachs. Dutton. ISBN 0-525-44605-2. TC '91.

An illustrious array of 34 authors and illustrators consider issues of peace and conflict from different viewpoints in short stories, poems, and songs.

🍎 Readers gained new insights into conflict and its resolution. The collection stimulated discussion on concern for peace, acknowledging diversity, taking a stand, and the genesis of conflict in both personal and global encounters.

Bill Peet: An Autobiography

Bill Peet. Illustrated by the author. Houghton Mifflin. ISBN 0-395-50935-7. TC '90.

> Bill Peet was raised in Indiana by his mother, a teacher. As a child, he drew cartoons in his school tablets and on the margins of his textbooks. After high school and art school he auditioned for the Disney studios and was hired as a cartoonist. He worked there for many years but always wanted to work on his own creations. When he was able to retire from Disney he began to create his own characters which children love.

> 🍎 Bill Peet fans were enthusiastic at finding out about their favorite illustrator. Budding artists took heart from the long struggle and persistence Bill Peet showed. Students used the storyboard technique to section out a play based on Bill Peet's life.

Bird Watch

Jane Yolen. Illustrated by Ted Lewin. Philomel. ISBN 0-399-21612-X. TC '91.

> A collection of 17 poems shows that birdwatching is no further away than the turn of a page. The book celebrates birds and displays them in their natural habitats through insightful poetry and vivid art. The beautiful word pictures provide a wealth of information.

> 🍎 This book led to a listing of "Birds I Know" followed by a day spent observing birds. Students wrote their own poetry and illustrated a class bird watch book.

The Black Snowman

Phil Mendez. Illustrated by Carole Byard. Scholastic. ISBN 0-590-40552-7. TC '90.

Through a blending of realism and fantasy, the author presents a powerful story that explores the moods, feelings, and relationships of two brothers who live in the inner city. Jacob and Peewee learn about their African heritage through the magic of a kente cloth they drape around a snowman fashioned from city snow. Byard's bold, sensitive illustrations add drama to this presentation of modern and historical black culture.

Students discussed Jacob's growth in self-esteem and pride in his heritage. The message (be proud of yourself and your ancestry) led to a study of multicultural literature. Students searched for books that conveyed their own heritage.

Buffalo Hunt

Russell Freedman. Holiday House. ISBN 0-8234-0702-0. TC '89.

This magnificent informational book traces the historical role of the buffalo in Native American life and folklore. Museum reproductions of famous paintings enrich Freedman's sensitive portrayal of the animals that were the mainstay of life for Native Americans.

Native American lifestyle in relation to the buffalo became the focal point of study in several classrooms. One student made a poster with a buffalo in the center surrounded by the uses made of it. Some researched songs and chants glorifying the buffalo and made their own books of buffalo songs.

Christopher Columbus: Voyager to the Unknown

Nancy Smiler Levinson. Illustrated with photos. Lodestar. ISBN 0-525-67292-3. TC '91.

This biography incorporates the most recent research including the controversy over Columbus's exact landing, describes each of his four voyages, and gives details of the aftermath of his discoveries.

🍎 This book was used in geography classes to study the early maps on what Columbus actually discovered. Discussion centered around such issues as where Columbus really landed and where he thought he was. The book became a model for use in writing workshops.

Clambake

Russell M. Peters. Illustrated with photos by John Madama. Lerner. ISBN 0-8225-2651-4. TC '93.

> The appanaug or clambake is a traditional ceremony of the Wampanoag Indians who live along the New England coast. This spectacular photographic essay shows Steven and his grandfather preparing for this gathering of friends and relatives.
>
> 🍎 Students will enjoy the historical value of these Native Americans and how they celebrate traditions. Information given here may lead to research on other aspects of Native American heritage.

Come Back, Salmon

Molly Cone. Illustrated with photos. Sierra Club. ISBN 0-87156-572-2. TC '93.

> Who says one school can't make a big difference in the fight to save the earth? Molly Cone chronicles the events that changed a dying river back to a salmon spawning ground, thanks to the efforts of students and teachers at Jackson Elementary School in Everett, Washington. Photographs help to capture the excitement, and sidebars provide important facts about the salmon life cycle. This book will inspire anyone willing to take on an ecological challenge.
>
> 🍎 After reading this book students wanted to begin a project immediately, but realized it would take considerable research, thought, and time. Subsequently, they formed groups and wrote up plans for an ecological project, which they presented first to their own class and then to the whole school. Presentations were well produced and included resources needed, timelines for completion, photographs, drawings, and even letters of support from the community.

© *Lerner Publications. Photograph by John Madama from* Clambake.

The next stage will be to implement those projects that received greatest support. Also appropriate for **Advanced.**

The Facts and Fictions of Minna Pratt
Patricia MacLachlan. Harper and Row. ISBN 0-96-024117-9. TC '89.

A sparkling and humorous story about an endearing 11-year-old who yearns to have a mother who acts like other mothers. Through experiences with her friend Lucas, Minna learns to value the eccentricities of her own parents.

🐛 This book triggered a discussion with gifted students about family values and appreciation of parental support. Like Mrs. Pratt, some teachers posted cryptic notices on the bulletin board to stimulate discussion and encouraged students to compose letters to their heroes as Minna does to Mozart.

From Abenaki to Zuni: A Dictionary of Native American Tribes

Evelyn Wolfson. Illustrated by William Sauts Bock. Walker. ISBN 0-8027-6790-7. TC '89.

Sixty-eight North American Indian tribes are described in brief two and three page entries. Segments provide the phonetic spelling and meaning of the name of the tribes, their location, dwellings, food, clothing, and transportation.

🐛 This book was used as a reference tool for groups studying Native American life and culture. The maps, symbols, labeled drawings, bibliographies, glossary, and index invit-

Reprinted with permission of Four Winds Press, an imprint of Macmillan Publishing Company, from George and Martha Washington at Home *by Beatrice Siegel, illustrated by Frank Aloise. Illustration copyright © 1989 Frank Aloise.*

ed browsing and spontaneous reading about numerous tribal groups.

George and Martha Washington at Home in New York

Beatrice Siegel. Illustrated by Frank Aloise. Four Winds. ISBN 0-02-782721-6. TC '90.

A description of the personal and professional life of George and Martha Washington during the 16 months the nation's capital was in New York City. The account stresses the government activities, historical events, and social occasions during the Washingtons' residency in New York.

🍂 A period in U.S. history took on new meaning for students. They reenacted the first inauguration, celebrated its 200th anniversary, and compared it with recent inaugurations. Students drew maps of New York City in 1789 and compared them with current maps. They studied the buildings in Philadelphia that housed the capital for the next 10 years while a permanent capital was built along the Potomac River.

Georgia O'Keeffe (Portraits of Women Artists for Children—series)

Robyn Montana Turner. Illustrated with photos and reproductions. Little, Brown. ISBN 0-316-85649-5. TC '92.

Part of a new series on women artists, this biography conveys a sense of Georgia O'Keeffe's life, her work as an artist, and her place in the art world. O'Keeffe became an artist at a time when few women were encouraged to pursue artistic careers. Through full-color reproductions of her paintings, readers experience her use of color, shape, and form to convey powerful images of gigantic flowers, vibrant cityscapes, and the desert.

🍂 The book was used as part of a biography unit to broaden the type of biographies read and discussed by children. Teachers particularly noted the need for books on famous women to balance the overemphasis on men in both history books and biographies. One teacher used the book as part of a focus on artists and put out bright paints and large sheets

of paper for children to explore bold, color-filled paintings. The book could also be used in a unit on the Southwest or as part of a self-esteem focus to explore the theme of "be your own true self."

Good Queen Bess: The Story of Elizabeth I of England
Diane Stanley and Peter Vennema. Illustrated by Diane Stanley.
Four Winds. ISBN 0-02-786810-9. TC '91.

This biography of the strong-willed Elizabeth I of England shows her influence on religion and politics, exploration of the New World, growth of English power, support for Shakespeare, and other 16th century people and events.

🐛 Detailed illustrations of 16th century life, along with the succinct text, gave students research tidbits and provided comparisons for a variety of projects on English history, exploration and explorers (e.g., the settlement of Virginia, Sir Francis Drake), women in history, time lines developed in math classes, and art techniques and the illustration process.

Goodbye, Vietnam
Gloria Whelan. Knopf. ISBN 0-679-82263-1. TC '93.

Whelan has captured the emotional turmoil and sadness of a family leaving their homeland for freedom in another country, fleeing from all that is familiar and boarding a less than seaworthy boat for the journey to a country that has no room for them. Seen through the eyes of 13-year-old Mai, the experiences of the Tran family become real. This is a well written story of strength and determination as a refugee family works to build a new life.

🐛 This book helped students understand what refugee families go through. Newspaper and magazine articles demonstrated how many people find they must flee their native lands. A chalk line drawn in the classroom approximated the measurements of the boat in the story. Students all moved inside the lines and stayed there for a whole school day. Homework directions were given in another language and there was only one translator. The next day students discussed the experience and wrote a story about how they felt. Some students who had really been refugees shared their experiences and others asked parents and grandparents to tell about relocation. Students then discussed and wrote about how they felt newcomers should be treated. This was effective sensitivity training! Also appropriate for **Advanced**.

Hannah

Gloria Whelan. Illustrated by Leslie Bowman. Knopf. ISBN 0-679-81397-7. TC '92.

> This is a gentle story that focuses on a 9-year-old blind girl and her life in the West in 1887. Hannah is an interesting and sympathetic character. Her plight, being overprotected and overlooked, is addressed when the new teacher comes to board with the family and encourages them to help Hannah move toward independence by teaching her life and school skills. The realistic pencil drawings greatly enhance the book's appeal.
>
> 🐝 The text lends itself to the study of family and school life in the 1800s, the invention of Braille, and handicap awareness.

Her Seven Brothers

Paul Goble. Illustrated by the author. Bradbury. ISBN 0-02-737960-4. TC '89.

> The Cheyenne Indian legend of the creation of the Big Dipper is retold in lyric prose and interpreted in dazzling illustrations. A sense of Native Americans' respect for the earth and sky pervades the folkloric rendition.
>
> 🐝 Science, social studies, art, music, drama, and folklore study all grew from this slender book. The ecological issues related to the environment created a sense of respect for Native American views of the land and sky.

I, Columbus: My Journal 1492-93

Edited by Peter Roop and Connie Roop. Illustrated by Peter E. Hanson. Walker. ISBN 0-8027-6978-0. TC '91.

> Based on the log translated by Robert H. Fuson, this exciting story is as amazing as Christopher Columbus himself. The end pages include copies of maps showing his voyage to the New World and return home.
>
> 🐝 This book breathed new life into social studies units on exploration. Students enjoyed the first-hand account and were interested in the journal format. It prompted discussions about sources of historical information and methods for gathering historical data.

If You Made a Million

David M. Schwartz. Illustrated by Steven Kellogg. Lothrop, Lee & Shepard. ISBN 0-688-07018-3. TC '90.

A description of how we get money and what we can do with it, this book shows the various forms money can take including coins, paper money, and personal checks. It also shows how money can be used to make purchases, to pay off loans, and to build interest in a bank.

❦ Students used this book to develop concepts about money and economics. They did research on currency in various countries and made charts of comparable values in money systems. They wrote about how a million dollars would change their lives, whether it was possible to have too much money, and the complicated life of a millionaire.

Insect Metamorphosis: From Egg to Adult

Ron Goor and Nancy Goor. Illustrated with photos. Atheneum. ISBN 0-689-31445-0. TC '91.

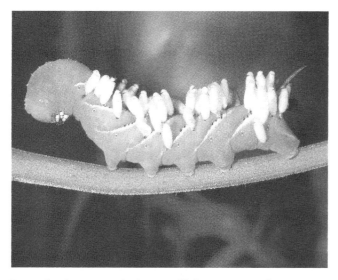

Reprinted with permission of Atheneum Publishers, an imprint of Macmillan Publishing Company, from Insect Metamorphosis *by Ron and Nancy Goor. Illustrations copyright © 1990 Ron and Nancy Goor.*

Stunning photographs and intriguing text unite to provide accurate information about the development of various types of insects.

🐛 Field trips led children to become more skilled in observation and identification of insects. The descriptive language coupled with the close-up photos inspired children to discuss their ideas about the beauty of nature. Older students conducted in-depth research on insects.

Inside the Whale and Other Animals

Steve Parker. Illustrated by Ted Dewan. Doubleday. ISBN 0-385-30651-2. TC '93.

This marvelously inventive introduction to animal anatomy and internal design will appeal to readers and book browsers of all ages. Portions of the skeletons, circulatory systems, and the major internal organ systems of 21 animals are shown in colorful cross sections. The main focus of each two-page spread is the drawing, which appears in the center and covers most of the space. The text keyed to the drawings is clearly written and provides fascinating facts about the animals and their environment.

🐛 This book was used as a tie-in with *The Voyage of the Mimi* and other ecological units. It was used as an introduction to bones and the anatomy of several types of animals. Great resource book for research projects in the intermediate grades. Also appropriate for **Advanced.**

Jeremy Thatcher, Dragon Hatcher

Bruce Coville. Illustrated by Gary A. Lippincott. ISBN 0-15-200748-2. TC '92.

Jeremy has been entrusted with raising a baby dragon that only he can see. Through the dragon, Jeremy, an aspiring artist, is encouraged to think in pictures. An enticing plot filled with humor and suspense creates a strong fantasy story. Debates between Jeremy and his friends about the merits of specific young adult authors are interspersed throughout the story line.

🐛 Readers were encouraged to recognize and use their natural abilities and imaginations as the connection between visual imagery and story was fostered. Readers also embarked on author studies in an effort to determine their own favorite authors.

The King's Day: Louis XIV of France

Aliki. Illustrated by the author. Crowell. ISBN 0-690-04588-3. TC '90.

A day in the life of flamboyant King Louis XIV of France who loved ceremony, ritual, and elegant clothes as much as life. The palace at Versailles was the king's favorite residence. Accompanied by courtiers, he strolled its expansive gardens. Sometimes the public was invited to watch him while he dined.

🦋 Students charted a time line of King Louis's day using French words when possible. They listed characteristics of the king and collaborated to write a biographical poem about him. They compared his lifestyle with that of today's leaders and compared a contemporary child's life with that of a child in King Louis XIV's time.

The King's Equal

Katherine Paterson. Illustrated by Vladimir Vagin. HarperCollins. ISBN 0-06-022496-7. TC '93.

This is not a revisionist fairy tale. It retains the old form (a prince who cannot marry until he finds a bride equal to himself), but it adds depth of character and invention that would make Cinderella envious. Paintings reveal a kingdom where the quest is worth the effort, and the book is appropriately bound in gold.

🦋 Select one scene that will serve as a preview to this book. Have a narrator provide enough detail to make the scene comprehensible. Have students perform the scene, using dialogue in the text and adding their own. Play the scene several times and evaluate. This drama tie-in should enrich transaction with the book. Also appropriate for **Primary.**

Klara's New World

Jeanette Winter. Illustrated by the author. Knopf. ISBN 0-679-80626-1. TC '93.

Klara's family struggles to make a good life in Sweden. Their plot of land is poor, there has been a drought, and they're running out of food. Klara must go to work for the lord of the manor, even though she is only 8 years old. After her parents receive a letter from America describing the beautiful, fertile, plentiful land, Klara knows she will be leaving behind everything she loves, even her grandfather.

Students can discuss how changes in lifestyle, surroundings, and family can affect their personal lives forever. The book also provides an introduction to reading other stories about immigrants and the problems immigrants deal with. Also appropriate for **Primary.**

The Last Princess: The Story of Princess Ka'iulani of Hawai'i
Fay Stanley. Illustrated by Diane Stanley. Four Winds. ISBN 0-02-786785-4. TC '92.

As its history is revealed in this book, Hawaii becomes more than a mysterious, enchanting place. This is also the tragic and courageous story of Princess Ka'iulani, who was born to rule that island kingdom.

❧ In addition to launching a study of Hawaiian history, the book was used as a discussion springboard for ideas such as women's issues, monarchy, prejudice, and loyalty. This question sparked a lively debate. Did foreigners have the right to come to Hawaii and take over forcefully?

Let Freedom Ring
Myra Cohn Livingston. Illustrated by Samuel Byrd. Holiday House. ISBN 0-8234-0957-0. TC '93.

Myra Cohn Livingston, renowned poet, tells the story of Martin Luther King, Jr.'s life in a ballad. She uses quotes from Dr. King's sermons and speeches. "From every mountainside, let freedom ring" illustrates his vision of a world in which all people, regardless of color, can live side by side in peace.

❧ Students can see through verse and pictures the reflections of a powerful person who touched many lives in this century. The book may lead them to search for more information about King's life and the historical context for his remarkable achievements. Also appropriate for **Advanced**.

Little John and Plutie
Pat Edwards. Houghton Mifflin. ISBN 0-395-48223-2. TC '89.

In a story set in the rural South in 1897, 9-year-old Little John meets Plutie, a cheerful black boy who does odd jobs at Grandmother's boarding house. The boys develop a strong friendship despite restrictive social conventions and racial prejudice of the time.

❧ This honest look at racial prejudice in the South of 1897 stimulated intense discussions about conditions then

and now. Recent news stories were compared with the problems that Little John and Plutie faced and led to students writing news stories about the story characters.

Living with Dinosaurs

Patricia Lauber. Illustrated by Douglas Henderson. Bradbury. ISBN 0-02-754521-0. TC '92.

> Give this book to all resident dinosaur experts and watch pairs of eyes light up! This journey of 75 million years back in time involves readers in the fascinating story of life as it was then. The book goes beyond dinosaurs, too, describing land formations, geography, and natural history, including many species of animals that lived around and among the dinosaurs and were part of the ecosystem. A complete index with pronunciation guide is included.

🐛 Children made a chart listing Dinosaurs/Not Dinosaurs, adding information from other sources as well. Teachers brought in fossils for children to examine, and then the class made "fossils" (available in kit form from many science supply catalogs). Environments and predator/prey relationships were discussed.

Manatee on Location

Kathy Darling. Illustrated with photos by Tara Darling. Lothrop, Lee & Shepard. ISBN 0-688-09030-3. TC '92.

For millions of years the manatee has lived in the shallow coastal seas and waterways of Florida. Kathy and Tara Darling, a mother-daughter team, "lived" with the manatees and dedicated the book to the saving of this part of U.S. national heritage.

🐛 This is an excellent book for the scientific study of an endangered species in such trouble that there are only 1,200 remaining in the world. Children were particularly interested in the photographs and the research done by the author and photographer.

Photograph by Tara Darling © 1991 from Kathy Darling's Manatee.
Reprinted by permission of Lothrop, Lee & Shepard Books, a division of William Morrow & Company, Inc.

Mojave

Diane Siebert. Illustrated by Wendell Minor. Crowell. ISBN 0-690-04569-7. TC '89.

Siebert's evocative and poetic text, extended by Minor's spectacular paintings, explores the land and animals of the Mojave Desert in a celebration of the wonders of nature. Descriptions of arroyos as streams of tears dried by the sun, tumbleweed as stumbling and bumbling, and mountain ranges creasing the desert's face with frowns and smiles create lasting images.

🍎 Teachers probed this book from several perspectives. From a literary view, they encouraged students to discuss how point-of-view, personification, and figurative language intertwined to create memorable images. From a scientific view, they examined vocabulary unique to the desert, studied the plant and animal adaptations to the environment, and discussed ecological issues. From an aesthetic view, they discussed how the textual and visual images combined to create a memorable experience.

My Daniel

Pam Conrad. Harper & Row. ISBN 0-06-021313-2. TC '90.

Ellie and Stevie learn about a family legacy when their 80-year-old grandmother, Julia Creath Summerwaite, comes to visit. Julia, eager to take the children to the Natural History Museum, interweaves the museum visit with flashbacks about her brother Daniel's historical quest for dinosaur bones on their Nebraska farm.

🍎 Teachers used the competition among paleontologists for dinosaur bones to extend the study of the westward movement, pioneers, the Homestead Act, and early day farming. Some groups recreated a model of the dinosaur excavation and collected fossils for an exhibit. Others wrote a concluding chapter to the open-ended story.

My Grandmother's Stories: A Collection of Jewish Folk Tales

Adele Geras. Illustrated by Jael Jordan. Knopf. ISBN 0-679-80910-4. TC '91.

This is a collection of 10 Jewish folktales told to a child by her grandmother, each inspired by an ordinary object or family treasure found in the house.

❦ The stories prompted many discussions on topics ranging from wisdom and foolishness to Jewish customs and traditions, cultural differences and similarities, and the relationship between the grandmother and granddaughter. A great book for reading aloud.

Number the Stars

Lois Lowry. Houghton Mifflin. ISBN 0-395-51060-0. TC '90.

During the Nazi occupation of Denmark in 1943, when Danish Jews were being sent to concentration camps, 10-year-old Annemarie learns to be brave. Her family helps her Jewish friend escape while Annemarie discovers that bravery means not thinking of the dangers she has to face, but just doing what is necessary at the moment.

❦ Students searched for other books describing humanitarian efforts during World War II, such as *Rescue* by Milton Meltzer. They studied maps of Denmark and Sweden to locate the setting of the story. They discussed this book as a welcome addition to Holocaust literature.

On Top of the World: The Conquest of Mount Everest

Mary Ann Fraser. Illustrated by the author. Henry Holt. ISBN 0-8050-1578-7. TC '92.

Edmund Hillary and Tenzing Norgay became the first men to reach the summit of Mount Everest on May 29, 1953. The danger and the drama of the climb, as well as the teamwork of the two men, is beautifully captured in this account for young readers.

❦ Children are extremely interested in adventure and the excitement associated with famous men and women. This book offers material to satisfy that curiosity. It was read over and over by children interested in stories of courage and conquering the unknown.

Paul Revere's Ride

Henry Wadsworth Longfellow. Illustrated by Ted Rand. Dutton. ISBN 0-525-44610-9. TC '91.

Ted Rand's visual interpretation of Longfellow's classic poem re-creates Paul Revere's ride in 1775, which warned the people around Boston that the British army was coming.

🐾 This book was used in social studies units dealing with the American Revolution; American literature, especially Longfellow and his poetry; and biographical information on Paul Revere and other patriots. Detailed maps on the endpapers show the routes taken by Revere, Dawes, and Prescott. Student projects included choral readings and dramatic presentations of the poem; reports on the small details of life such as clothing styles, methods of communication, and transportation; research opportunities to create biographies of the people of 1775; and use of watercolor illustrations in reports and biographies.

Pueblo Boy: Growing Up in Two Worlds

Marcia Keegan. Illustrated with photos by the author. Cobblehill. ISBN 0-525-65060-1. TC '92.

Timmy is a 10-year-old Pueblo Indian boy whose life in a New Mexico pueblo is a mixture of contemporary American culture and Native American traditions. The clear, colorful photographs follow Timmy in his daily life as he interacts with other tribal members in learning the customs and ceremonies of his ancestors.

🐾 This book is particularly important in providing children with a picture of contemporary Pueblo Indian life. Many teachers incorporated the book into studies of the Southwest and of Pueblo Indian tribes. In one classroom, the book was used with other photographic essay books showing the daily lives of children from Inuit and Latino cultures. After exploring these books in small group discussions, the children gathered stories of their own family traditions and wrote books showing how those traditions were part of their daily lives.

Pueblo Storyteller

Diane Hoyt-Goldsmith. Illustrated with photos by Lawrence Migdale. Holiday House. ISBN 0-8234-0864-7. TC '92.

The contemporary life of a young Cochiti girl in a New Mexico pueblo is told through a well written text and color photographs. As she learns tribal traditions such as making loaves of bread, sculpting the Storyteller figures, making Cochiti drums, and dancing the Buffalo Dance, she collects the memories of her life and people to pass on to future generations.

Like *Pueblo Boy,* this book is an excellent resource on modern life in Native American communities in the Southwest. The focus on storytelling led one class to explore the many ways in which groups of people tell stories, including story knives and story boards. They also interviewed grandparents and other family members about their own family stories and storytelling traditions.

Ragtime Tumpie

Alan Schroeder. Illustrated by Bernie Fuchs. Joy Street/Little, Brown. ISBN 0-316-77497-9. TC '90.

A fictionalized account of the childhood of Josephine Baker, the St. Louis dancer who became the toast of Paris. Tumpie, as Baker was called as a child, won a silver dollar in a dance contest in 1915 and determined that she would become an entertainer.

Josephine Baker's story was read during Black History Month as a role model of a person who worked hard to fulfill her dream. The music teacher played the music provided on the endpapers to give students a sense of ragtime. Josephine Baker was added to a time line in the study of famous black Americans.

The Riddle of Penncroft Farm

Dorothea Jensen. Gulliver/HBJ. ISBN 0-15-200574-9. TC '90.

Sixth grader Lars Olafson resents his family's move to Great-Aunt Cass's Penncroft Farm in Pennsylvania. Despite his aunt's enthusiasm for the farm and its history, Lars remains aloof until he meets Geordie, the ghost of an 18th-century boy who recounts his adventures near Penncroft Farm during the American Revolution. The juxtaposition of time involves the reader in solving a modern-day mystery while learning about the historical period.

❦ Teachers discussed the literary techniques Jensen uses to personalize the past, to show different points of view, and to carry multiple story lines. They discussed Jensen's suggestion that "the Revolutionary War was America's first Civil War." They discussed the division of families, located the riddles in the story, and studied the Colonial terminology and monetary systems of Revolutionary times.

A River Ran Wild
Lynne Cherry. Illustrated by the author. Gulliver/HBJ. ISBN 0-15-200542-0. TC '93.

Once upon a time and long ago, many rivers ran wild through lands of towering forests. But "progress" and "invention" sometimes change the environment we so easily take for granted. Lynne Cherry looks at the history of a New England river and describes the deterioration of a once pristine environment with both words and illustrations.

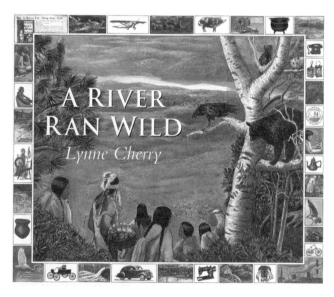

Courtesy of Harcourt Brace & Company. Copyright © 1992 Lynne Cherry. Reproduced by permission.

People who lived alongside the river were convinced that their commitment to a "sparkling river" was possible and began efforts to change regulations and laws that contributed to the pollution. Here is a story where "one person can make a difference."

❧ Useful in studying the conflict between "progress" and the environment in science and history units. Also appropriate for **Primary** and **Advanced**.

Riverkeeper

George Ancona. Illustrated with photos. Macmillan. ISBN 0-02-700911-4. TC '91.

John Cronin, an environmentalist, is a caretaker of the Hudson River in New York. Through graphic photographs and text, the author describes Cronin's unusual career and mission to clean the river and catch polluters.

❧ This book's emphasis on environmental preservation made it a favorite for science and social studies classes. Teachers used it in a study of careers in environmental fields.

Rocks and Minerals

R.F. Symes and the staff of the Natural History Museum, London. Illustrated with photographs by Colin Keates. Alfred A. Knopf Books for Young Readers. ISBN 0-394-99621-6. TC '89.

This book incorporates information in text and illustration on major classifications of rocks, their uses, rock forming minerals, gemstones, ores, metals, collecting, and cutting rocks and minerals.

❧ Students used this book to identify the types of rocks and minerals they found for their own collections. They discussed the effect of certain rocks and minerals on the economic and social development of a region, e.g., the effect of gold in South Africa. They created their own fact books about rocks and minerals.

The Samurai's Daughter
Robert D. San Souci, reteller. Illustrated by Stephen T. Johnson. Dial. ISBN 0-8037-1135-2. TC '93.

This is a beautiful retelling of a Japanese legend. Tokoyo is a strong female character who is determined to contribute to the Samurai virtues of courage, endurance, and the warrior's duty to protect the weak—even as she is taught to be ladylike and genteel. When her beloved father is exiled, Tokoyo sets out to find him, climbing mountains, crossing the ocean, and battling a sea serpent. The story deals with ideas specific to the Japanese Samurai lifestyle and culture. Lovely pastel paintings support and enhance the text.

🐛 Teachers used the book in folklore units and also in discussions about Japanese history and customs, geography, and women's issues.

Sarah Morton's Day: A Day in the Life of a Pilgrim Girl
Kate Waters. Illustrated by Russ Kendall. Scholastic. ISBN 0-590-42634-6. TC '90.

We are invited to share the daily activities of Sarah Morton, a young interpreter at the Plimoth Plantation, a living history museum in Plymouth, Massachusetts. The color photo essay allows us to see the details of early morning, chore time, recreation, learning, and family life with Sarah, her mother, and her new father in the year 1627.

🐛 Teachers used this as an excellent introduction to the Colonial period, ca. 1600-1775. Students made Indian cornbread, traced the meanings of words listed in the glossary, and compared this book with others about Plimoth Plantation. They used the author's notes to verify the authenticity of information in the photographs.

Sierra
Diane Siebert. Illustrated by Wendell Minor. HarperCollins. ISBN 0-06-021639-5. TC '92.

This collaborative effort is a fine poetic and artistic tribute to the Sierra Nevada mountain range. The volume celebrates the animals that reside in the timber and boulders of this range. Cycles of life and the seasons are featured.

🍏 Some teachers focused on climatology, using the book to help children understand weather patterns. Science and ecology of the food chains were also studied. Art students studied the realistic animal portraits and used that information in a study of acrylics. Movements of the earth and the study of geology could also be undertaken, using this book as a resource.

The Sierra Club Book of Great Mammals
Linsay Knight. Illustrated with photos and art. Sierra Club. ISBN 0-87156-507-2. TC '93.

> After opening with a brief overview of mammals, this book focuses on the larger mammals in a text filled with interesting facts. Excellent photographs and illustrations invite children into the mammals' world.
>
> 🍏 It was used to encourage research on mammals. Charts were made listing the animal, habitat, food, enemies, and special traits. Students worked in groups to create a mural with different types of animals in separate areas. Small groups focused on one animal, comparing information, reading poetry and stories, and searching for folklore that portrayed their animal in a special way.

Skeleton
Steve Parker. Illustrated with photographs by Philip Dowell. Alfred A. Knopf Books for Young Readers. ISBN 0-394-99620-8. TC '89.

> In a photo essay format that provides a visual feast, Parker presents a study of the evolution, structure, and function of human and animal skeletal systems. Brilliant photographs based on museum collections have a three dimensional quality.
>
> 🍏 The science and health study applications were quickly made by students and teachers alike. One group made models of the skeletal forms; another drew diagrams of human and animal forms.

Summer of Fire: Yellowstone 1988

Patricia Lauber. Illustrated with photos. Orchard. ISBN 0-531-05943-X. TC '92.

Yellowstone National Park was burning in the summer of 1988. This fire in Wyoming, Montana, and Idaho was not the only hot spot; a controversy raged in Washington regarding fire fighting policies as well. Some agencies held that fire was a rebirth, and others wanted to fight the fire with maximum effort. This volume shows the growth after a fire and benefits of fire such as the fact that the Lodgepole pine tree needs fire in order to reseed.

🍎 In science, teachers used this in a unit on reseeding, ecosystems, and wildlife habitats. In math, teachers used the figures to show cost of fighting fires and numbers of trees in a given quadrant. For students in lower grades, the glossary of terms was used for vocabulary extension.

Talking with Artists

Pat Cummings, compiler and editor. Illustrated with photos and art. Bradbury. ISBN 0-02-724245-5. TC '93.

This collection invites children into the lives and thoughts of their favorite artists, 14 picture book illustrators. Each segment contains an autobiographical essay, photographs of the illustrator as a child and as an adult, samples of early and current artistic efforts, and responses to an identical set of questions about each person's work.

🍎 The use of the same questions for each interview allows children to make comparisons across illustrators and see the many ways in which they can go about creating illustrations. This book is an invitation for children to find their own way of using art to tell stories about their lives as well as a reference source for illustrator studies in the classroom. Also appropriate for **Primary** and **Advanced**.

Why Do Our Bodies Stop Growing?

Dr. Philip Whitfield and Dr. Ruth Whitfield. Viking Kestrel. ISBN 0-670-82331-7. TC '89.

The title question is only the beginning of an adventure for students as they gain answers to this and other questions about human anatomy, such as "Why do I get goose bumps?" This informational text is the third in a series based on questions asked by staff at the Natural History Museum.

🐛 Health conscious teachers and students turned to this reference book repeatedly to learn about their bodies. Some used it as a model for creating their own books about themselves. Others used the book as a springboard for research into physical phenomena.

Wind in the Long Grass: A Collection of Haiku
William J. Higginson, ed. Illustrated by Sandra Speidel. Simon & Schuster. ISBN 0-671-67978-3. TC '92.

The poems in this book are presented in such a way that the movement from season to season is evident. The haiku that are included come from many parts of the world. Some are in the traditional pattern, but others are more loosely formed.

🐛 The collection offers material to enrich units on poetry or on multicultural literature. The emphasis on word choice in haiku leads naturally to descriptive writing activities.

Windows on Wildlife
Ginny Johnston and Judy Cutchins. Illustrated with photos. Morrow. ISBN 0-688-07873-7. TC '91.

This book examines six natural habitat exhibits in the U.S. and focuses on the technical aspects of constructing the exhibits. It also showcases the feeding habits and care of young animals.

🐛 Science students used this as a supplemental text to study mammals, reptiles, and amphibians. The book also became part of a unit on occupations in science and the focus of environmental and ecological studies.

Advanced
(Grades 6-8)

Ancient Egypt
George Hart. Illustrated with photos by Peter Hayman. Knopf.
ISBN 0-679-90742-4. TC '91.

This photo/text overview of life in ancient Egypt includes descriptions of daily life and work, societal ideas and ideals, religious beliefs, education, entertainment, and other events as documented by clothing, sculpture, artwork, mummies, and other objects that have survived. Part of the Eyewitness series.

❦ With hundreds of illustrations and a fact-filled text, this book makes numerous comparisons between life today and in ancient Egypt: food, clothing, shelter, religion, methods of warfare, buildings, transportation, medicine, and writing processes are just a few of the topics presented. The book is excellent for browsing but the information and illustrations can be incorporated into reports (written in hieroglyphics perhaps) and used for bulletin boards, dramatic costumes and plays, and other teacher/student created projects.

And One for All
Theresa Nelson. Orchard. ISBN 0-531-08404-3. TC '90.

Thirteen-year-old Geraldine's close relationship with her older brother, Wing, and his friend Sam changes when Wing joins the Marines to fight in Vietnam and Sam leaves for Washington to join a peace march. Geraldine's story provides a kaleidoscopic view of issues of conflicting loyalties and the Vietnam War.

🐝 Teachers discussed the author's technique of using Geraldine's bus ride to Washington to reorder the events of the past two years. As her views and understanding change, so do the reader's. The students discussed the struggle, values, beliefs, and divisions created during the Vietnam War. Students compared *Across Five Aprils* and *My Brother Sam Is Dead* and the tension created when members of a family disagree about a war. They discussed the use of metaphors of snakes, color, and carved initials as effective images. They discussed the use of letters from Wing written from Vietnam and the changes in voice and tone with the differences in Geraldine's perspective.

Anthony Burns: The Defeat and Triumph of a Fugitive Slave

Virginia Hamilton. Alfred A. Knopf Books for Young Readers. ISBN 0-394-98185-5. TC '89.

A deeply moving biography of an escaped slave from Virginia who was captured in Boston in 1854, arrested, tried, and subsequently returned to slavery through questionable legal maneuvers. The compelling drama helps readers to identify strongly with Anthony Burns and to see life as he saw it through poignant flashbacks of his life as a slave.

🐝 This book was examined for its skillful literary structure, tension, and controlled passion. Students valued the helpfulness of a list of people involved in Burns's life story provided at the front of the book and used the technique in their own writing. The connections to a study of the U.S. Civil War, slavery, moral issues, constitutional law, and politics of that period are apparent.

Bard of Avon: The Story of William Shakespeare

Diane Stanley and Peter Vennema. Illustrated by Diane Stanley. Morrow. ISBN 0-688-09108-3. TC '93.

Fact versus fiction...what do we really know about the most famous playwright ever born? The writers approach historical research like detectives, being careful to help readers understand the differences between verifiable and "probable"

Illustration © 1992 by Diane Stanley from Bard of Avon *by Diane Stanley and Peter Vennema. Reprinted with permission from Morrow, Junior Books, a division of William Morrow & Co.*

details about Shakespeare's life and times. Richly illustrated pages give insight into the colorful Elizabethan England that supported the talent of a gifted writer.

🍂 This text will be usable for intermediate through high school students. A postscript adds valuable and interesting information about the language of Shakespeare's time.

Bearstone
Will Hobbs. Atheneum. ISBN 0-689-31496-5. TC '90.

Cloyd, a Navajo-Ute Indian youth, struggles with personal and cultural identity. After growing up without parents, he encounters one more white authority figure—an old widowed rancher. When Cloyd is sent to spend the summer with him, he considers running back to the rugged Utah/Colorado mountains where his grandmother lives. However, exploring a cave above the ranch, he discovers a small turquoise bear, and in Ute tradition gives himself a new name, Lone Bear. With the bearstone as his talisman Cloyd begins to prove his worth.

🍂 Students studied the setting of the story by locating it on maps and in pictures of the geography of the Colorado-Utah plateau and the Continental Divide. They compared traditions of the Navajo and Ute Indian tribes and investigated other animals deemed sacred by Native Americans. A deep respect for the land and protection of its inhabitants correlated with Earth Day activities. Students identified with Cloyd's challenges and reactions and discussed their own adult-youth conflicts and resolutions.

The Borning Room

Paul Fleischman. Zolotow/HarperCollins. ISBN 0-06-023762-7.
TC '92.

In this novel of cycles of births and deaths, the life of an Ohio farm girl in the late 1800s is told through scenes occurring in the family's borning room. The joys and hardships of Georgina's life within a warm, close family are set against the changing world issues of runaway slaves, war and peace, women's suffrage, religion, and education. The two themes of strong family values and the social and political change in the United States are effectively intertwined in this short but powerful novel.

🐛 Teachers and children wanted to read and discuss this novel with others because of its depth and complex issues. One teacher read it aloud to introduce a broad focus on cycles and followed that with various units throughout the school year. Many found it an effective addition to studies of pioneer life, the Civil War, slavery, women's studies, life and death cycles, and families' stories. In one classroom, children made time lines of significant places and events in their lives.

Breaking the Chains: African-American Slave Resistance

William Loren Katz. Illustrated with prints and photos.
Atheneum. ISBN 0-689-31493-0. TC '91.

Using primary source material, Katz contradicts the widely accepted myths about slavery in the U.S.—that African-Americans were satisfied with their lot and did little to free themselves. The book includes little known facts of history such as the alliance between blacks and Native Americans.

🐛 The book fills a gap in the materials needed for the study of the institution of slavery and increases one's knowledge of and respect for those who were brought to America in chains. Excellent for study of the history of the U.S. Civil War, Black History Month, research on black awareness, and as a comparison with novels such as *The Red Badge of Courage* and *Anthony Burns: The Defeat and Triumph of a Fugitive Slave*.

Chingis Khan

Demi. Illustrated by the author. Henry Holt. ISBN 0-8050-1708-9. TC '92.

Based on history and legend, this is a fascinating story of a young Mongol boy who faced overwhelming odds to become supreme master of the largest empire ever created in the lifetime of one man. The exquisite illustrations enhance the presentation.

🎭 Teachers used this biography with students to study cultures, to develop visual literacy, and to contrast China's peoples. They also found it a good basis for comparison with legends of other countries, for discussing political issues, and for the study of this author/illustrator.

The Dark Thirty: Southern Tales of the Supernatural

Patricia C. McKissack. Illustrated by Brian Pinkney. Knopf. ISBN 0-679-81863-4. TC '93.

Spine-tingling and hair-raising tales of African-American storytelling tradition, from days of slavery to civil rights, are collected in this edition to share with eager young listeners. The black and white scratchboard illustrations add eeriness.

🎭 Teachers can use these tales for prediction, for imagery, or for character study. Students will be enticed to write tales based on events that border on the unexplainable. Also appropriate for **Intermediate.**

The Drackenburg Adventure

Lloyd Alexander. Dutton Children's Books. ISBN 0-525-44389-4. TC '89.

Alexander says he wanted to give Vesper Holly, the central character also in *The Illyrian Adventure* and *The El Dorado Adventure,* a quiet holiday, but some unforeseen developments occur. In 1873 17-year-old Vesper and her guardians travel to an obscure European grand duchy, where their archenemy is plotting its annexation by a neighboring kingdom while he pursues a lost art treasure. Naturally, high-spirited Vesper Holly lands in the middle of an outrageous escapade.

🍂 Alexander dedicated the book to "Vespers past, present, and future," so the strong female protagonist became the subject of discussion as a role model. Students discussed the entire trilogy, including the author's placement of this adventure, its relation to preceding books, new characters, and newly discovered explanations. They also discussed the fantasy elements of magical powers and a created land. They compared this trilogy with Alexander's Westmark trilogy and his Prydain series for similarities among characters and events. They discussed Alexander as a writer and evaluated his books according to his own statement: "The writer is not a monarch but a subject. Characters must appear plausible in their own setting. Details should be tested for consistency."

Franklin Delano Roosevelt

Russell Freedman. Illustrated with photos. Clarion. ISBN 0-89919-379-X. TC '91.

Photographs and text effectively portray Franklin Delano Roosevelt as an athletic young man who rose to the U.S. presidency despite paralysis from polio.

🍂 This book was an excellent resource for a cross-curricular study of the Great Depression era. Readers gained keen insight into an important period of American history while also recognizing the scientific and technological advances made since then. This readable biography helped students focus on one man's life against the backdrop of the times in which he lived.

Gonna Sing My Head Off! American Folk Songs for Children

Kathleen Krull, collector and arranger. Illustrated by Allen Garns. Knopf. ISBN 0-394-81991-8. TC '93.

This collection of 62 American folk songs celebrates the diversity of peoples, regions, and time periods in the United States. Each song has a brief historical note and an illustration and includes music for both piano and guitar. The author notes that these songs "speak of ideals, changing the

Illustrations © 1992 Allen Garns.

world, good times, hard times, love, community, and the triumph of good over evil."

❧ The most obvious response to this book is to sing! Because of the historical notes, the songs can be integrated into other themes such as the study of a particular region or time. The song titles are listed alphabetically, by type, and by first line, making it easy to use the collection. Also appropriate for **Intermediate** and **Primary.**

The Great American Gold Rush

Rhoda Blumberg. Illustrated with photographs. Bradbury. ISBN 0-02-711681-6. TC '90.

A well researched chronicle of the emigration of people from the East Coast of the U.S. and from other countries to California to pursue the dream of discovering gold, 1848-1852. Numerous quotes from primary sources (diaries and letters) bring the spirit of the Forty-Niners to life and show the impact of gold fever on people.

❦ Students used the maps, chapter notes, and bibliography to study this memorable period of history and compared it with the gold rush that occurred in the Klondike. They discussed inflation, supply and demand, modes of transportation, crime and punishment, and other social problems generated by gold rush phenomena. Students in Utah compared what was happening in California with experiences in Utah during the same period. They discussed the propaganda technique of luring Argonauts to the gold fields and discussed figurative language related to gold.

The Great Little Madison

Jean Fritz. Illustrated with photographs. Putnam. ISBN 0-399-21768-1. TC '90.

Jean Fritz continues her close personal look at historical figures in this biography of James Madison, the fourth president of the United States, father of the Constitution, and architect of the Bill of Rights. Although he was short of stature and small of voice, Madison's commitment to making the Constitution work was truly strong; he persuaded George Washington to appear at the Philadelphia writing and he influenced Thomas Jefferson on the Louisiana Purchase. Fritz takes her title from a note Dolley Payne Todd wrote to a friend saying that "the great little Madison has asked to be brought out to see me this evening."

❦ Students needed background information to understand Madison's impact on historical events and written documents. Teachers made a time line of events in Madison's life and listed parallel events in Europe and Asia to gain an international perspective. One class drew a mural of battles in the War of 1812, the burning of Washington D.C., the writing of the "Star Spangled Banner," Jackson's victory at New Orleans, and the signing of the Treaty of Ghent. Map study, mock trials, dramatizations, and research into Dolley Madison's dress and hairstyles followed reading.

How It Feels to Fight for Your Life

Jill Krementz. Photographs by the author. Joy Street/Little, Brown. ISBN 0-316-50364-9. TC '90.

Fourteen courageous children, ages 8 to 16, detail their physical and emotional fight against severe medical problems. The youngsters tell their own stories about battles with pain, uncertainty, and the changes brought about by cancer, severe burns, asthma, and kidney failure.

This book served as an impetus for journal writing; it fostered recollection and reflection. It became a springboard to discussions in science and social studies focused on advancements in medicine, complexities of life, frailty of human beings, and each person's unique ability to confront difficult situations.

The Igloo

Charlotte Yue and David Yue. Illustrated by the authors. Houghton Mifflin. ISBN 0-395-44613-9. TC '89.

Igloos fascinate nearly everyone and yet they are only one of the clever adaptations the Eskimo people have made to their harsh environment. The Yues describe Eskimo customs, house building, hunting, sleds, clothing, food preparation, traveling, and life today.

The bibliographies led students to pursue an entire unit of study on Eskimo life that included science projects, social studies, art, music, and drama.

Inca and Spaniard: Pizarro and the Conquest of Peru

Albert Marrin. Illustrated with prints. Atheneum. ISBN 0-689-31481-7. TC '90.

Marrin describes the rise of the rich and powerful Inca Empire and its fall to the ruthless Spanish conqueror Hernando Pizarro. As the so-called "Children of the Sun," the Inca were organized by the absolute lord, Sapa Inca, whose feet were never allowed to touch the ground. Each citizen was controlled in a precise place in society, but in turn the society protected its citizens.

🐛 History and social studies teachers used this book to study historical eras dealing with the rise of the Indian cultures in Peru and the effects of the Spanish conquest. Students discussed cultural clashes, colonialism, reasons for war, and causes and effects of a conquest, and compared similar events in recent history. Others made map studies of Central and South America, used primary resources from the text and illustrations, and examined biographies of Spanish conquerors. Students believed this book could promote pride for ESL students through an appreciation for their ethnic background.

Independence Avenue

Eileen B. Sherman. Jewish Publication Society. ISBN 0-8276-0367-3. TC '91.

This book examines the life of a Russian Jewish immigrant to the U.S. in 1907. Elias Cherovnosky must learn to adapt his Old World traditions to a new environment in Galveston, Texas. Working in American society was a real shock to a man who had to change everything, including his name.

🐛 This book was part of a study of immigrants and adaptation to a new environment. Students learned about American life at the turn of the century and the difficulties faced by Russian immigrants who came to escape oppression and poverty.

An Indian Winter

Russell Freedman. Illustrated with the art of Karl Bodmer. Holiday House. ISBN 0-8234-0930-9. TC '93.

This well researched book tells of the adventures of the German naturalist Prince Alexander Philipp Maximilian and the Swiss painter Karl Bodmer as they journeyed up the Missouri River and into Indian Country in 1833-34. The book focuses on the winter spent by the Prince and Bodmer with the Mandan and Hidatsa Indians. It provides a detailed journal, portraits, landscapes, drawings, and scenes of everyday life of Native Americans in a highly readable, interesting style.

❦ Teachers used this book as a model for journal writing, diaries, and as a multicultural resource in art, social studies, American history, and the history of bookmaking. Also appropriate for **Intermediate.**

Into the Mummy's Tomb

Nicholas Reeves. Illustrated with photos and drawings. Scholastic/Madison. ISBN 0-590-45752-7. TC '93.

Reeves tells of Lord Carnarvon and Howard Carter's exciting searches for King Tut's tomb in the 1920s and includes information about life in ancient Egypt. Numerous drawings and photographs, a glossary, description of how mummies were made, and a short list of recommended further readings are included.

❦ Students did alternative methods of reporting on the information they found by using acrostic poems of Tutankhamun's name and bio-poems. Some used the K-W-L strategy to learn about mummies. They compared information from other articles. Others went on to Egyptian myths or a study of hieroglyphics. Also appropriate for **Intermediate.**

Letters from a Slave Girl: The Story of Harriet Jacobs

Mary E. Lyons. Scribners. ISBN 0-684-19446-5. TC '93.

This is a captivating story of perseverance and injustice in the life of a slave girl, accurately based on Harriet Jacobs's 1861 autobiography. Before gaining her freedom Harriet endured seven years of confinement in a relative's storeroom. Her story, told through letters, gives a taste of dialect and expression of the time. Harriet displays a fierce spirit as she struggles with loneliness and illness in her captivity and sends a powerful message of the resiliency of African-American women.

❦ This book was used by sixth-grade students in comparing African-American slavery to German Occupation as revealed in *The Diary of Anne Frank.* Teachers and media generalists tried these activities with the book: Compare biography and autobiography. Which category fits the letters? Compare copies of *To Be a Slave* by Julius Lester to *Letters from a Slave Girl.* Lyons's book is catalogued as fiction and the Lester book is nonfiction. Determine why they are different. Prepare a historical outline of slavery in the United States. Highlight significant events. Compare the life of a slave from a man's perspective, then from a woman's perspective. Keep a journal for one month. Use Harriet's technique and address it to a family member or friend you don't see every day. Also appropriate for **Intermediate.**

Littlejim
Gloria Houston. Illustrated by Thomas Allen. Philomel. ISBN 0-399-22220-0. TC '91.

Twelve-year-old Littlejim and his abusive, illiterate father have very little in common. As this sensitive Appalachian child seeks the approval of his tough, uneducated father, he ponders, "What does it mean to be a man?" This tale of a young boy growing up is also about a grown man's maturing.

Students kept response journals as they read. They studied the contrasts between the man and the boy, between life during the World War I period and today, and between cultures.

Ludie's Song
Dirlie Herlihy. Dial Books for Young Readers. ISBN 0-8037-0533-6. TC '89.

In rural Georgia in the late 1950s, 13-year-old Martha becomes friends with artistically gifted Ludie, who is black and has been disfigured in a fire. Martha discovers that although Ludie is intelligent, warm hearted, and talented, these qualities do not matter to people who are prejudiced. Dangers arise for both families because of the friendship.

Blatant racism, prejudice, and the need for the civil rights movement became meaningful to students as they discussed this book. Current news items of discrimination were compared with events of the 1950s.

Lyddie

Katherine Paterson. Lodestar. ISBN 0-525-67338-5. TC '92.

This is a wonderful story of perseverance and personal growth set in a Massachusetts fabric mill in the 1840s. It focuses on Lyddie, a factory girl, and vividly depicts her experiences there. Lyddie displays a fierce spirit as she struggles with loneliness, loss, illness, and illiteracy, but she survives and overcomes these major adversities. The carefully researched story presents a little known piece of 19th century life with rich descriptions that make it memorable.

🍎 When they finished reading this novel, upper grade students developed a character map. The purpose was to focus on the main characters in the book, identifying qualities or traits on the basis of their actions in the story.

My Name Is Not Angelica

Scott O'Dell. Houghton Mifflin. ISBN 0-395-51061-9. TC '90.

Raisha, a young African, and her family are captured and transported to the Danish Virgin Islands in the 1730s. She describes the slave revolt on St. John's Island and tells how she and other runaways coped with the brutal treatment meted out by plantation owners and the colonial government. When the revolutionaries are faced with recapture and choose to die instead, Raisha, always the survivor, protects her unborn child and opts for life and the hope of a better existence in the future.

🍎 The book stimulated discussions of people's inhumane treatment of one another and the responses of the oppressed.

Nothing to Fear

Jackie French Koller. HBJ. ISBN 0-15-200544-7. TC '92.

New York City during the Great Depression comes alive through the experiences of young Daniel Garvey, the son of Irish immigrants. Vivid descriptions create believable scenes from that period; more important, they characterize the feelings of the people who lived each day with a sense of desperation, not knowing where the next meal would come from. At first, Daniel is only aware of poor people begging on the streets; before long, his own family is suffering because of his father's unemployment. The ending of this tale of hardship lightens the tone of the book but keeps the historical period well in perspective.

❧ Students found it interesting to survey their community for evidence of economic difficulties, noting such signs as homeless people, lines at food banks, and an increase in real estate for sale. They were also encouraged to recall family stories about immigration and survival in a new country.

The Painter's Eye: Learning to Look at Contemporary American Art
Jan Greenberg and Sandra Jordan. Illustrated with photos. Delacorte. ISBN 0-385-30319-X. TC '92.

Through conversations with the artists, the authors take readers on an exciting exploration of modern art. Extensive photographs of paintings and artists at work add a special dimension to the journey. Readers connect with the artists and their work as a special web is woven.

❧ Readers can explore the work of various artists and their techniques and become familiar with the "language of art" as they read this book.

Park's Quest
Katherine Paterson. Lodestar. ISBN 0-525-67258-3. TC '89.

Parkington Waddell Broughton the Fifth is 11 years old, lives with his mother in Washington, D.C., and on this particular Veterans Day wants to know more about his father, who was killed in Vietnam. His quest for his legacy, intermingled with the Arthurian legend that Park rehearses in his fantasies, leads him to his grandfather and a Vietnamese half sister.

❧ The emotionally gripping story forced students to face uncomfortable realities about Vietnam, family entanglements, and the need for love and acceptance. The blend of the King Arthur legend took students back to that story as they discussed parallels with its modern day counterpart.

71

People Who Make a Difference

Brent Ashabranner. Illustrated with photographs by Paul Conklin. Cobblehill/Dutton. ISBN 0-525-65009-1. TC '90.

A collection of short biographies about people who are doing things to make the world around them a better place to live. They include a Dallas policeman who helps Southeast-Asian refugees, an 83-year-old woman who saves endangered species of sea turtles, a woman who helps paroled women offenders, and a Capuchin friar who organized a housing program for the homeless.

🍎 This book showed students that one person can make a difference and led to discussions of life, work, and commitment. It became a stimulus to considerations of social history and personal values.

The Place My Words Are Looking For

Paul Janeczko, compiler. Bradbury. ISBN 0-02-747671-5. TC '91.

This unique anthology contains outstanding poetry as well as minibiographies in which 40 poets share their personal experiences and emotions about writing poetry. Janeczko invited a variety of poets to express what it means to be a poet and to explore different poetic styles by discussing the themes and intentions underlying their work. Among others, Myra Cohn Livingston discusses loneliness, X.J. Kennedy explains how he finds his poetic ideas, and Jim Daniels depicts a negative encounter during childhood as the inspiration for poetry.

🍎 This book was an inspiration to young writers and poets. Students realized that they, too, are capable of writing poetry when they understand how poets shape experiences from their lives. The book was a stimulus to the study of poetry, poetic styles, and the people behind the poems.

Red Cap

G. Clifton Wisler. Lodestar. ISBN 0-525-67337-7. TC '92.

Ransom Powell, 13 years old and just four feet tall, left home to serve the Union Army as a drummer boy in 1862. After two years he was captured and taken to a Confederate prison in Andersonville, Georgia. Ransom, nicknamed

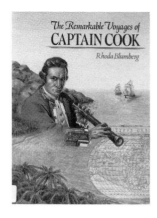

Cover illustration from Rhoda Blumberg's
The Remarkable Voyages of Captain
Cook *reprinted by permission of Jonathan Hunt.*

"Red Cap" by fellow soldiers was befriended by a
Confederate guard and given the job of camp drummer boy.
The story offers a view of the terrible cost of war as seen
through the eyes of a young boy who believes strongly in
his cause.

☙ Students charted a time line of the American Civil War
and the length of time Red Cap was in prison. They listed
the variety and amount of food they ate for a week and
compared their lists with the rations allotted the prisoners.
They studied maps of Virginia, Maryland, and Georgia to
get a sense of the location and geography of the Civil War.

The Remarkable Voyages of Captain Cook

Rhoda Blumberg. Illustrated with prints. Bradbury. ISBN 0-02-
711682-4. TC '92.

This fine book draws the reader into the drama of Captain
Cook's explorations. There is opportunity to see preserved
artwork by artists who traveled with him and, while reading about history, to see its effect on those who lived during
that period.

☙ Teachers used this book in a social studies explorer unit
and to provide information about the discovery of Hawaii,
Australia, New Zealand, and other areas of the Pacific. In
one school, the book became the stimulus for a play about
Hawaii.

Rescue: The Story of How Gentiles Saved Jews in the Holocaust

Milton Meltzer. Harper and Row. ISBN 0-06-024210-8. TC '89.

Rescue focuses on the humanitarian acts of individuals and groups of Gentiles who risked their lives to save Europe's Jews from certain death during the Holocaust. Among the stories, Meltzer describes the rescue of almost all of Denmark's 7,700 Jews through the organized efforts of many Danish citizens. Raoul Wallenberg's heroic acts to save thousands of Hungarian Jews and the stories of others who rescued Jews in Poland, France, Italy, and Germany are also recounted.

❦ This excellent addition to Holocaust literature gave students a different perspective from which to compare other fictional and nonfictional accounts they have read. It restored some of their faith in humankind. The book was used to study World War II, the Holocaust, humanitarianism, and the need for international peace.

Rice Without Rain

Minfong Ho. Lothrop, Lee & Shepard. ISBN 0-688-06355-1. TC '91.

Contemporary life in Thailand is described in a story rich with contrasts and an exploration of values and the need for change. Jinda leaves her native village to join a political protest in Bangkok but returns to the land.

❦ Students developed charts to contrast aspects of rural and urban life in Thailand with that in the United States. Cooperative learning groups focused on topics such as the treatment of women, the importance of family relationships, personal responsibilities, political upheaval, and change. Research groups explored student uprisings in Thailand, the U.S., and China.

Rising Voices: Writings of Young Native Americans

Arlene B. Hirschfelder and Beverly R. Singer, selectors. Scribners. ISBN 0-684-19207-1. TC '93.

The poems and essays in this collection are statements by more than 60 young people. Their words reveal deep feelings about their proud heritage and the sadness they feel about the treatment of Native People in the United States. Hope for a better future brings a sense of optimism to the writing. Each piece by itself is thought provoking.

❦ This volume stands alone as a selection of prose and poetry, but it is also a valuable resource for the study of Native Americans, contemporary as well as historical. Students may be encouraged to try both poetry and essay forms to express their own pride of heritage and their observations about the quality of life they see today and hope to see in the future. Also appropriate for **Intermediate.**

The Road to Memphis
Mildred D. Taylor. Dial. ISBN 0-8037-0340-6. TC '91.

Cassie Logan and her brothers, from *Roll of Thunder, Hear My Cry,* and *Let the Circle Be Unbroken,* continue the saga of life for black Americans in the 1940s. This story of discrimination and coming of age encourages reflective thinking.

❦ The book was excellent for stimulating discussions of race relations, the U.S. civil rights movement, fear and courage, the value of education, and self-concept. Student writing evolved from the following questions: What does the car represent to Cassie and the young men before and after the trip? How do decisions affect the lives of the characters? What family or personal decision changed the course of your life?

Ryan White: My Own Story
Ryan White and Ann Marie Cunningham. Illustrated with photos. Dial. ISBN 0-8037-0977-3. TC '92.

After Ryan, a 13-year-old hemophiliac, contracted AIDS through tainted blood products, he was denied the right to return to his school. In this touching, yet realistic book Ryan White described his legal battle to return to school. His courageous spirit was evident as he became a spokesman for issues concerning this deadly disease.

❦ The book was used in science and health classes to study courage, values, and prejudices. Teachers found it a great discussion opener.

Sculpture: Behind the Scenes

Andrew Pekarik. Illustrated with photos. Hyperion. ISBN 1-56282-294-2. TC '93.

> "Art is an experience, not a thing" (p. 10), states the author, who questions and probes to help readers experience sculpture from almost everywhere, displaying clear photos of Picasso's cardboard-and-string guitar, Degas's wax dancer, Calder's "Hanging Spider," and many others—a bountiful collection.
>
> ❧ After this book is read and responded to, try a quickwrite. Students view a sculpture from all angles, touch or handle it if possible, and then jot down their liveliest impressions. Then, working together, they combine parts of these quickwrites into a free verse reflecting their aesthetic experience. Also appropriate for **Intermediate.**

A Selection from the Canterbury Tales

Retold by Selina Hastings. Illustrated by Reg Cartwright. Henry Holt and Company. ISBN 0-8050-0904-3. TC '89.

> The great narrative poem, *The Canterbury Tales,* was written by Geoffrey Chaucer in the late 14th Century and consists of 24 tales told by a group of pilgrims as they travel from London to Canterbury Cathedral. Seven tales are retold here.
>
> ❧ This book was read aloud as an early introduction to the works of Chaucer. Teachers compared the modern prose retelling with samplings from an Old English version and from *Canterbury Tales* (selected, translated, and adapted by Barbara Cohen, illustrated by Trina Schart Hyman. Lothrop, 1988). This led to discussion of how language changes. Students tried to express their ideas in Old English.

Shabanu: Daughter of the Wind

Suzanne Fisher Staples. Knopf. ISBN 394-84815-7. TC '90.

> Survival for the nomadic tribes of the Cholistan Desert is a desperate struggle, especially in a time of drought; but the difficult life has not quenched the liveliness of 11-year-old Shabanu. Older sister Phulan will soon marry the wealthy

Hamir, Dadi will sell 15 good camels for excellent prices, and the dancing camel Guluband will bring extra money at the fairs to help tide the family through their problems. But the happy plans are wrecked, and Dadi pledges young Shabanu to marry the brother of a wealthy but despised landowner. By accepting her father's decision, Shabanu would bring prestige and survival for her family but would consign herself to a life of servitude and bondage. Her decision, as based on centuries of Pakistani tradition, is emotionally and intellectually challenging.

❦ Shabanu provides a rich base of information for comparisons of cultures, especially the role of women in society and expectations for young adults. The Cholistani culture is beautifully portrayed, and the book does refer to coming of age topics, including menstruation and mating, but the writing is discreet and essential to the story. Topics for comparison include impact of desert weather and geography on life, camels as economic products, and relationships of family members to one another and to traditional values. The author's skill in writing must be emphasized, for as one reviewer said, "The author paints pictures with words that stay in the reader's mind over time."

Shadow Shark
Colin Thiele. Harper and Row. ISBN 0-06-026179-X. TC '89.

Joe lives with Uncle Harry, Aunt Ellen, and cousins Meg and Maureen in Southern Australia. While swimming, the three adolescents narrowly escape a huge shark, known as old Scarface. The town hires a highly skilled amateur fisherman to get rid of the shark and Joe and Maureen go along to help in the galley. A tense battle ensues.

❦ The geography of the setting, Australia, became an item of interest as students located the scenes from the story and discussed other books set in the same area. The biggest interest came from students' comparisons with *Jaws,* a film they had all seen.

Shiloh
Phyllis Reynolds Naylor. Atheneum. ISBN 0-689-31614-3. TC '92.

Photograph from Barbara Rogasky's Smoke and Ashes: The Story of the Holocaust *reprinted by permission of Holiday House.*

This heartwarming, emotional novel focuses on a rural West Virginia boy and his dog. A gripping account of family conflict and honesty, the story offers an ethical dilemma about property rights vs. animal rights, and the reader is left to decide which to support.

❦ The story stimulated discussions about relationships, values, abuse, regional dialect, and economics. Some related activities were a visit from the Animal Humane Society, which included live animals and information about pet care, and a Pet Week, when students were able to bring in their own pets and share with classmates the pet's needs and the responsibility of being an owner.

Smoke and Ashes: The Story of the Holocaust
Barbara Rogasky. Holiday House. ISBN 0-8234-0697-0. TC '89.

Six million people were killed between 1933 and 1945, the years of the Holocaust, when the Nazis under the leadership of Adolf Hitler tried to exterminate all Jews. Chilling photographs and statistics, discussed in gripping prose, contemplate these unexplainable times.

✸ This book became a classroom resource used throughout the study of World War II. Students, unwilling to accept the brutality of the situation, were forced to acknowledge man's inhumanity to man.

Sojourner Truth: Ain't I a Woman?
Patricia C. McKissack and Fredrick McKissack. Illustrated with photos. Scholastic. ISBN 0-590-44690-8. TC '93.

This clearly written biography tells the story of a former slave who took the name Sojourner Truth to symbolize her willingness to speak powerfully against slavery anywhere to anyone who would listen. Sojourner Truth fought for her own freedom and that of her five children in the "free" northern U.S., even taking on the courts when her son was illegally sold south. She was a preacher, an abolitionist, and activist for the rights of blacks and women.

✸ The original photographs, documents, excerpts from her journal, and short biographical sketches encouraged

Copyright © 1992 by Patricia McKissack. Photograph/illustration reprint permission given by Scholastic.

children to pursue their own research. They were especially interested in primary sources such as slave diaries and the artwork and spirituals during that era as well as documents related to the women's suffrage movement. Also appropriate for **Intermediate.**

Songs of the Wild West
Commentary by Alan Axelrod. Music arranged by Dan Fox. Simon & Schuster. ISBN 0-671-74775-4. TC '92.

Forty-five songs combined with art from the Metropolitan Museum of Art, New York, and the Buffalo Bill Historical Center, Cody, Wyoming, are featured in this volume. Jaunty tunes and classic ballads highlight the Old West as portrayed by artists Frederic Remington, Charles M. Russell, and N.C. Wyeth, among others. The commentary helps establish the history of each song chosen for inclusion. The intriguing presentation makes it a temptation to hum the melody and stop to read each verse of a song.

This book is a music teacher's dream. The arrangements are fairly easy to read and the pages also give background information about the songs. Art teachers used the book to study the styles of Remington and Russell. History teachers used it to study artifacts of the Old West and their uses.

Sorrow's Kitchen: The Life and Folklore of Zora Neale Hurston
Mary E. Lyons. Illustrated with photos. Scribner's. ISBN 0-684-19198-9. TC '91.

This biography interweaves excerpts from the writing of Zora Neale Hurston along with the story of her life. Hurston, part of the Harlem Renaissance of the 1920s, wrote stories, plays, and articles that revealed aspects of her life and those around her during the migration of thousands of blacks from the American South to northern cities.

This biography was in great demand during Black History Month and in a study of women writers. It also served as the focus of a study of folklore and culture of Hurston's native U.S. South and the West Indies.

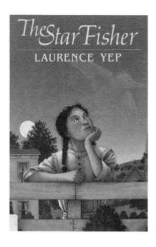

Illustration by Laurence Yep © 1991 from his The Star Fisher. *Reprinted by permission of Morrow Junior Books, a division of William Morrow & Company, Inc.*

The Star Fisher

Laurence Yep. Morrow. ISBN 0-688-09365-5. TC '92.

Chinese-American Joan Lee is 15 years old when she and her family leave Ohio in 1927 and move to West Virginia to open their own business. Joan must make friends at a new school, act as an interpreter for her family, accept adult responsibilities, and adapt to living in a town where some don't want her family. Laurence Yep's grandparents owned a laundry in West Virginia, and he blended many stories from his family into this book.

❧ This led into an author study with students rereading Yep's books and reading his biography, *The Lost Garden*. Many discussions centered around prejudice and growing up in two worlds.

Steal Away

Jennifer Armstrong. Orchard. ISBN 0-531-05983-9. TC '93.

Susannah, a white orphan, and Bethlehem, a slave assigned to her, together seek freedom from a Virginia farm in 1855. The 13-year-old girls' escape is recounted 41 years later as they tell their story to two other 13-year-old girls. Beneath the surface, readers sense a tension and a mystery as to why Susannah and Bethlehem do not end up living in the same geographic areas. This is a strong story of courage and emotions.

🐛 From a historical perspective, this book generates discussion about the Underground Railroad and the moral issues of slavery. Other significant themes include friendship and generational issues. Also appropriate for **Intermediate.**

The Voyage of the Frog

Gary Paulsen. Orchard. ISBN 0-531-05805-0. TC '90.

At 14, David Alspeth has learned the basics of sailing from his Uncle Owen. Upon Owen's unexpected death, David sails the 22-foot boat *Frog* into the Pacific to scatter his uncle's ashes onto the ocean. However, a freak storm leaves David and the *Frog* adrift; he encounters sharks and killer whales, is becalmed for days, and faces the terrible uncertainty of survival. His voyage on the *Frog* becomes a life-changing rite of passage.

🐛 Paulsen demonstrates his powerful crafting of taut survival stories that encourage profound discussions and response by young adults. The book generated questions dealing with the purposes of life, the meaning of death, courage and survival against great odds, and other universal topics. Science topics included whales and sharks, weather and ocean storms, sailing techniques, boating lore, and map readings in ocean travel. For literature, the book illustrates a marvelous adventure story told from a teenager's point of view, providing a basis for comparison with other titles in the genre.

What Hearts

Bruce Brooks. Laura Geringer/HarperCollins. ISBN 0-06-021131-8. TC '93.

Asa at age 6 triumphantly arrives home from his last day in kindergarten only to find that his life has taken a turn—divorce, a move, and a new stepfather. Asa at age 9, after yet another move, chooses between the spotlight in a class performance and loyalty to a new friend. Asa at 11 explores the intricacies of baseball and of his stepfather. Asa at 12 discovers that loving someone can be a growing, learning experience despite the pain. Bruce Brooks weaves together four short stories to offer a perceptive picture of Asa's developing sense of self from the inside out.

❧ In small groups students discussed Asa's feelings in each of the four stories. They then developed an emotional timeline for themselves, including events that had had a major impact on them. Each student selected one event from his/her timeline, drew a concept web of the feelings involved, and then wrote a short story about that event.

Where the Broken Heart Still Beats
Carolyn Meyer. Gulliver/HBJ. ISBN 0-15-200639-7. TC '93.

As a young girl, Cynthia Parker is captured by Comanche Indians and integrated into the tribe. She later marries and becomes the mother of the future Comanche Chief Quanah Parker. This story opens when she is recaptured by Texas Rangers 25 years later, in 1861. The story structure alternates between her cousin Lucy Parker's journal entries about Cynthia's unhappiness and attempts to escape, and the factual information about Comanche community life and the life of Texas settlers in the late 1800s.

❧ This book and *Quanah Parker: Comanche Chief* by Rosemary K. Kissinger (Pelican, 1991) are an excellent pair for partner reading. Another suggestion is to develop a timeline of historical events in Texas and in other parts of the U.S. during this time. A comparison investigation of other American captives might be of interest to some middle school students. Also appropriate for **Intermediate**.

Woodsong
Gary Paulsen. Illustrated by Ruth Wright Paulsen. Bradbury. ISBN 0-02-770221-9. TC '91.

An autobiographical account of the author's reflections on the peculiarities and surprises of nature and his thoughts and actions during his participation in the grueling 1,180-mile Iditarod dogsled race across Alaska.

❧ Student discussions centered around the natural order, survival, the beauty and terror of nature, the Iditarod race, and the loyalty and determination exemplified by the dogs and the author. Students related the book to Jack London's *The Call of the Wild* and *White Fang*.

Photograph from Russell Freedman's The Wright Brothers. How They Invented the Airplane. *Reprinted by permission of Holiday House.*

The Wright Brothers: How They Invented the Airplane

Russell Freedman. Illustrated with photos by Wilbur and Orville Wright. Holiday House. ISBN 0-8234-0875-2. TC '92.

This is a well researched biography of the Wright Brothers, beginning when they wrote to the Smithsonian Institution in Washington, D.C., for all the information available about everything from flight experiments to the world's first powered, sustained, and controlled airplane flight. The original photographs by Wilbur and Orville add to the presentation, and the many quotes from diaries, letters, and journals bring these famous brothers to life for the reader.

🍂 Students made a time line depicting the early history of flight. It became part of a study of the early 1900s. Another group discussed the Wrights' problem-solving approach and persistence. Some students chose to read about other inventors and compared their problem-solving approaches.

Author and Illustrator Index

Alexander, Lloyd. *The Drackenburg Adventure.* (1989). 62-63
Aliki. *The King's Day: Louis XIV of France.* (1990). 43
Allen, Thomas (Illustrator). *Littlejim.* (1991). 69
Allen, Thomas B. (Illustrator). *Going West.* (1993). 11
Aloise, Frank (Illustrator). *George and Martha Washington at Home in New York.* (1990). 36, 37
Ancona, George. *Riverkeeper.* (1991). 53
Armstrong, Jennifer. *Steal Away.* (1993). 81-82
Ashabranner, Brent. *People Who Make a Difference.* (1990). 72
Axelrod, Alan. *Songs of the Wild West.* (1992). 80

Baker, Leslie (Illustrator). *All Those Secrets of the World.* (1992). 3
Bash, Barbara. *Urban Roosts: Where Birds Nest in the City.* (1991). 26
Berenzy, Alix. *A Frog Prince.* (1990). 10
Bloom, Lloyd (Illustrator). *Yonder.* (1989). 29
Blumberg, Rhoda. *The Great American Gold Rush.* (1990). 65
____. *The Remarkable Voyages of Captain Cook.* (1992). 73
Blythe, Gary (Illustrator). *The Whales' Song.* (1992). 28
Bock, William Sauts (Illustrator). *From Abenaki to Zuni: A Dictionary of Native American Tribes.* (1989). 36-37
Bodmer, Karl (Illustrator). *An Indian Winter.* (1993). 67-68
Booth, Barbara D. *Mandy.* (1992). 16, 17
Bowman, Leslie (Illustrator). *Hannah.* (1992). 40
Brooks, Bruce. *What Hearts.* (1993). 82-83

85

Brown, Marcia, and Leo Dillon, Diane Dillon, Richard Egielski, Trina
    Schart Hyman, Maurice Sendak, Marc Simont, and Margot Zemach
    (Illustrators). *Sing a Song of Popcorn.* (1989). 21-22
Brown, Mary Barrett (Illustrator). *Great Northern Diver: The Loon.*
    (1991). 11-12
Bruchac, Joseph, and Jonathan London (Retellers). *Thirteen Moons on
    Turtle's Back.* (1993). 23-24
Bunting, Eve. *The Wednesday Surprise.* (1990). 27
____. *The Wall.* (1991). 27
____. *Fly Away Home.* (1992). 9
Byam, Michele. *Arms and Armor.* (1989). 30
Byard, Carole (Illustrator). *The Black Snowman.* (1990). 33
Byrd, Samuel (Illustrator). *Let Freedom Ring.* (1993). 45, 46

Carle, Eric. *A House for Hermit Crab.* (1989). 12
____ (Illustrator). *Eric Carle's Animals Animals.* (1990). 8
Carr, Jan (*see* de Regniers, Beatrice Schenk)
Carrick, Donald (Illustrator). *The Wednesday Surprise.* (1990). 27
Cartwright, Reg (Illustrator). *A Selection from the Canterbury Tales.*
    (1989). 76
Chall, Marsha W. *Up North at the Cabin.* (1993). 24-26
Cherry, Lynne. *The Great Kapok Tree: A Tale of the Amazon Rain Forest.*
    (1991). 11
____. *A River Ran Wild.* (1993). 52-53
Cole, Joanna. *The Magic School Bus Inside the Human Body.* (1990). 16
Cone, Molly. *Come Back, Salmon.* (1993). 34-35
Conklin, Paul (Illustrator). *People Who Make a Difference.* (1990). 72
Conrad, Pam. *My Daniel.* (1990). 48
Cooney, Barbara (Illustrator). *The Year of the Perfect Christmas Tree.*
    (1989). 28-29
Coville, Bruce. *Jeremy Thatcher, Dragon Hatcher.* (1992). 42-43
Cummings, Pat (Illustrator). *Storm in the Night.* (1989). 22-23
____ (Compiler and Editor). *Talking with Artists.* (1993). 56
Cunningham, Ann Marie (*see* White, Ryan)
Cutchins, Judy (*see* Johnston, Ginny)

Darling, Kathy. *Manatee on Location.* (1992). 47
Darling, Tara (Illustrator). *Manatee on Location.* (1992). 47
Davie, Helen K. (Illustrator). *The Star Maiden: An Ojibway Tale.* (1989). 22
Day, Edward C. *John Tabor's Ride.* (1990). 13-14
de Regniers, Beatrice Schenk, Eva Moore, Mary Michaels White, and
    Jan Carr. *Sing a Song of Popcorn.* (1989). 20-21
Degen, Bruce (Illustrator). *The Magic School Bus Inside the Human Body.*
    (1990). 16

Taylor, Mildred D. *The Road to Memphis*. (1991). 75
Thiele, Colin. *Shadow Shark*. (1989). 77
Turner, Robyn Montana. *Georgia O'Keeffe (Portraits of Women Artists for Children—series)*. (1992). 37-38

Vagin, Vladimir (Illustrator). *The King's Equal*. (1993). 43
Van Leeuwen, Jean. *Going West*. (1993). 11
Vennema, Peter (*see* Stanley, Diane)
Vivas, Julie (Illustrator). *Let the Celebrations Begin!* (1992). 15

Waters, Kate. *Sarah Morton's Day: A Day in the Life of a Pilgrim Girl*. (1990). 54
Wells, Rosemary. *Forest of Dreams*. (1989). 9-10
Whelan, Gloria. *Hannah*. (1992). 40
___. *Goodbye, Vietnam*. (1993). 39
Whipple, Laura. *Eric Carle's Animals Animals*. (1990). 8
White, Mary Michaels (*see* de Regniers, Beatrice Schenk)
White, Ryan, and Ann Marie Cunningham. *Ryan White: My Own Story*. (1992). 75
Whitfield, Dr. Philip, and Dr. Ruth Whitfield. *Why Do Our Bodies Stop Growing?* (1989). 56-57
Whitfield, Dr. Ruth (*see* Whitfield, Dr. Philip)
Wild, Margaret. *Let the Celebrations Begin!* (1992). 15
Winter, Jeanette. *Klara's New World*. (1993). 44
Winthrop, Elizabeth. *Vasilissa the Beautiful*. (1992). 26
Wisler, G. Clifton. *Red Cap*. (1992). 72-73
Wisniewski, David. *Rain Player*. (1992). 19
Wolfson, Evelyn. *From Abenaki to Zuni: A Dictionary of Native American Tribes*. (1989). 36-37
Wright, Wilbur and Orville (Illustrators). *The Wright Brothers: How They Invented the Airplane*. (1992). 84

Yep, Laurence. *The Star Fisher*. (1992). 81
Yolen, Jane. *Bird Watch*. (1991). 32
___. *All Those Secrets of the World*. (1992). 3
___. *Encounter*. (1993). 7-8
Yoshida, Toshi. *Young Lions*. (1990). 29
Young, Ed. *Seven Blind Mice*. (1993). 20-21
Yue, Charlotte, and David Yue. *The Igloo*. (1989). 66
Yue, David (*see* Yue, Charlotte)

Zalben, Jane Breskin (Illustrator). *Inner Chimes: Poems on Poetry*. (1993). 12-13
Zemach, Margot (*see* Brown, Marcia)
Zimmer, Dirk (Illustrator). *John Tabor's Ride*. (1990). 13-14

Title Index

Christopher Columbus: Voyager to the Unknown. Nancy Smiler Levinson. (1991). 33-34
Clambake. Russell M. Peters. (1993). 34, 35
Come Back, Salmon. Molly Cone. (1993). 34-35
The Dark Thirty: Southern Tales of the Supernatural. Patricia C. McKissack. (1993). 62
The Drackenburg Adventure. Lloyd Alexander. (1989). 62-63
Dragonfly's Tale. Kristina Rodanas (Reteller). (1993). 6
Dream Wolf. Paul Goble. (1991). 7
The Empty Pot. Demi. (1991). 7
Encounter. Jane Yolen. (1993). 7-8
Eric Carle's Animals Animals. Laura Whipple. (1990). 8

The Facts and Fictions of Minna Pratt. Patricia MacLachlan. (1989). 35-36
Feathers for Lunch. Lois Ehlert. (1991). 8-9
Fly Away Home. Eve Bunting. (1992). 9
Forest of Dreams. Rosemary Wells. (1989). 9-10
Franklin Delano Roosevelt. Russell Freedman. (1991). 63
A Frog Prince. Alix Berenzy. (1990). 10
From Abenaki to Zuni: A Dictionary of Native American Tribes. Evelyn Wolfson. (1989). 36-37

George and Martha Washington at Home in New York. Beatrice Siegel. (1990). 36, 37
Georgia O'Keeffe (Portraits of Women Artists for Children—series). Robyn Montana Turner. (1992). 37-38
Going West. Jean Van Leeuwen. (1993). 11
Gonna Sing My Head Off! American Folk Songs for Children. Kathleen Krull (Collector and Arranger). (1993). 63-64
Good Queen Bess: The Story of Elizabeth I of England. Diane Stanley and Peter Vennema. (1991). 38, 39
Goodbye, Vietnam. Gloria Whelan. (1993). 39
The Great American Gold Rush. Rhoda Blumberg. (1990). 65
The Great Kapok Tree: A Tale of the Amazon Rain Forest. Lynne Cherry. (1991). 11
The Great Little Madison. Jean Fritz. (1990). 65-66
Great Northern Diver: The Loon. Barbara Juster Esbensen. (1991). 11-12

Hannah. Gloria Whelan. (1992). 40
Her Seven Brothers. Paul Goble. (1989). 40
A House for Hermit Crab. Eric Carle. (1989). 12

How It Feels to Fight for Your Life. Jill Krementz. (1990). 66
I, Columbus: My Journal 1492-93. Peter Roop and Connie Roop (Eds.). (1991). 40
If You Made a Million. David M. Schwartz. (1990). 41
The Igloo. Charlotte Yue and David Yue. (1989). 66
Inca and Spaniard: Pizarro and the Conquest of Peru. Albert Marrin. (1990). 66-67
Independence Avenue. Eileen B. Sherman. (1991). 67
An Indian Winter. Russell Freedman. (1993). 67-68
Inner Chimes: Poems on Poetry. Bobbye S. Goldstein. (1993). 12-13
Insect Metamorphosis: From Egg to Adult. Ron Goor and Nancy Goor. (1991). 41-42
Inside the Whale and Other Animals. Steve Parker. (1993). 42
Into the Mummy's Tomb. Nicholas Reeves. (1993). 68
Is Your Mama a Llama? Deborah Guarino. (1990). 13

Jeremy Thatcher, Dragon Hatcher. Bruce Coville. (1992). 42-43
John Tabor's Ride. Edward C. Day. (1990). 13-14

The Keeping Quilt. Patricia Polacco. (1989). 14-15
The King's Day: Louis XIV of France. Aliki. (1990). 43
The King's Equal. Katherine Paterson. (1993). 43
Klara's New World. Jeanette Winter. (1993). 44

The Last Princess: The Story of Princess Ka'iulani of Hawai'i. Fay Stanley. (1992). 45
The Legend of the Indian Paintbrush. Tomie dePaola. (1989). 15
Let Freedom Ring. Myra Cohn Livingston. (1993). 45, 46
Let the Celebrations Begin! Margaret Wild. (1992). 15
Letters from a Slave Girl: The Story of Harriet Jacobs. Mary E. Lyons. (1993). 68-69
Little John and Plutie. Pat Edwards. (1989). 45-46
Littlejim. Gloria Houston. (1991). 69
Living with Dinosaurs. Patricia Lauber. (1992). 46-47
Ludie's Song. Dirlie Herlihy. (1989). 69
Lyddie. Katherine Paterson. (1992). 70

The Magic School Bus Inside the Human Body. Joanna Cole. (1990). 16
Manatee on Location. Kathy Darling. (1992). 47
Mandy. Barbara D. Booth. (1992). 16, 17
Mojave. Diane Siebert. (1989). 48
My Daniel. Pam Conrad. (1990). 48
My Grandmother's Stories: A Collection of Jewish Folk Tales. Adele Geras.

(1991). 48-49
My Great-Aunt Arizona. Gloria Houston. (1993). 16-17
My Name Is Not Angelica. Scott O'Dell. (1990). 70

Nothing to Fear. Jackie French Koller. (1992). 70-71
Number the Stars. Lois Lowry. (1990). 49

On Top of the World: The Conquest of Mount Everest. Mary Ann Fraser.
   (1992). 49
Osa's Pride. Ann Grifalconi. (1991). 17-18

The Painter's Eye: Learning to Look at Contemporary American Art. Jan
   Greenberg and Sandra Jordan. (1992). 71
Park's Quest. Katherine Paterson. (1989). 71
Paul Revere's Ride. Henry Wadsworth Longfellow. (1991). 50
People Who Make a Difference. Brent Ashabranner. (1990). 72
The Place My Words Are Looking For. Paul Janeczko (Compiler). (1991). 72
Princess Furball. Charlotte Huck. (1990). 18-19
Pueblo Boy: Growing Up in Two Worlds. Marcia Keegan. (1992). 50
Pueblo Storyteller. Diane Hoyt-Goldsmith. (1992). 51

Ragtime Tumpie. Alan Schroeder. (1990). 51
Rain Player. David Wisniewski. (1992). 19
Red Cap. G. Clifton Wisler. (1992). 72-73
The Remarkable Voyages of Captain Cook. Rhoda Blumberg. (1992). 73
Rescue: The Story of How Gentiles Saved Jews in the Holocaust. Milton
   Meltzer. (1989). 74
Rice Without Rain. Minfong Ho. (1991). 74
The Riddle of Penncroft Farm. Dorothea Jensen. (1990). 51-52
Rising Voices: Writings of Young Native Americans. Arlene B. Hirschfelder
   and Beverly R. Singer (Selectors). (1993). 74-75
Riverkeeper. George Ancona. (1991). 53
A River Ran Wild. Lynne Cherry. (1993). 52-53
The Road to Memphis. Mildred D. Taylor. (1991). 75
Rocks and Minerals. R.F. Symes. (1989). 53
The Rough-Face Girl. Rafe Martin. (1993). 19
The Rumor of Pavel and Paali: A Ukrainian Folktale. Carol Kismaric
   (Adapter). (1989). 20
Ryan White: My Own Story. Ryan White and Ann Marie Cunningham.
   (1992). 75

Sami and the Time of the Troubles. Florence Parry Heide and Judith Heide
   Gilliland. (1993). 20, 21

The Samurai's Daughter. Robert D. San Souci (Reteller). (1993). 54
Sarah Morton's Day: A Day in the Life of a Pilgrim Girl. Kate Waters. (1990). 54
Sculpture: Behind the Scenes. Andrew Pekarik. (1993). 76
A Selection from the Canterbury Tales. Selina Hastings. (1989). 76
Seven Blind Mice. Ed Young. (1993). 20-21
Shabanu: Daughter of the Wind. Suzanne Fisher Staples. (1990). 76-77
Shadow Shark. Colin Thiele. (1989). 77
Shiloh. Phyllis Reynolds Naylor. (1992). 77-78
Sierra. Diane Siebert. (1992). 54-55
The Sierra Club Book of Great Mammals. Linsay Knight. (1993). 55
Sing a Song of Popcorn. Beatrice Schenk de Regniers, Eva Moore, Mary Michaels White, and Jan Carr. (1989). 21-22
Skeleton. Steve Parker. (1989). 55
Smoke and Ashes: The Story of the Holocaust. Barbara Rogasky. (1989). 78, 79
Sojourner Truth: Ain't I a Woman? Patricia C. McKissack and Fredrick McKissack. (1993). 79-80
Songs of the Wild West. Alan Axelrod. (1992). 80
Sorrow's Kitchen: The Life and Folklore of Zora Neale Hurston. Mary E. Lyons. (1991). 80
The Star Fisher. Laurence Yep. (1992). 81
The Star Maiden: An Ojibway Tale. Barbara Juster Esbensen. (1989). 22
Steal Away. Jennifer Armstrong. (1993). 81-82
Storm in the Night. Mary Stolz. (1989). 22-23
Sukey and the Mermaid. Robert D. San Souci. (1993). 23
Summer of Fire: Yellowstone 1988. Patricia Lauber. (1992). 56

Talking with Artists. Pat Cummings (Compiler and Editor). (1993). 56
Thirteen Moons on Turtle's Back. Joseph Bruchac and Jonathan London (Retellers). (1993). 23-24
Thunder Cake. Patricia Polacco. (1991). 24
Totem Pole. Diane Hoyt-Goldsmith. (1991). 24

Up North at the Cabin. Marsha W. Chall. (1993). 24-26
Urban Roosts: Where Birds Nest in the City. Barbara Bash. (1991). 26

Vasilissa the Beautiful. Elizabeth Winthrop. (1992). 26
A Visit to Oma. Marisabina Russo. (1992). 26-27
The Voyage of the Frog. Gary Paulsen. (1990). 82

The Wall. Eve Bunting. (1991). 27
The Wednesday Surprise. Eve Bunting. (1990). 27
The Whales' Song. Dyan Sheldon. (1992). 28

The International Reading Association attempts, through its publications, to provide a forum for a wide spectrum of opinions on reading. This policy permits divergent viewpoints without assuming the endorsement of the Association.

Director of Publications Joan M. Irwin
Managing Editor Anne Fullerton
Associate Editor Romayne McElhaney
Assistant Editor Amy Trefsger
Editorial Assistant Janet Parrack
Production Department Manager Iona Sauscermen
Graphic Design Coordinator Boni Nash
Design Consultant Larry Husfelt
Desktop Publishing Supervisor Wendy Mazur
Desktop Publishing Anette Schütz-Ruff
Cheryl Strum
Richard James
Proofing David Roberts

Cover photo Mary Loewenstein Anderson

Also available from IRA...

If children read books they like, they will like to read. Here are three lists of books that have been tested and endorsed by the experts— real kids, teens, and teachers. These lists are a wonderful source for parents, teachers, and young readers alike. Children's Choices is a listing of new children's books that school children from across the U.S. chose as their favorites. Young Adults' Choices includes books selected by young adult readers as the ones they consider the most enjoyable and informative. Teachers' Choices identifies the new trade books for children and adolescents that classroom teachers consider to be exceptional in curriculum use. All lists include annotations and bibliographic information.

Booklists are available at the following rates:

10 copies	$5.00
100 copies	$40.00
500 copies	$150.00

To order your copies of Children's Choices, Young Adults' Choices, or Teachers' Choices, call 1-800-336-READ, ext. 266 (outside North America call 302-731-1600, ext. 266).

Children's Choices	No. 386-622
Young Adults' Choices	No. 387-622
Teachers' Choices	No. 388-622